Lives

PREFACE.

I do not doubt that there will be many,1 Atticus, who will think this kind of writing 2 trifling in its nature, and not sufficiently adapted to the characters of eminent men, when they shall find it related who taught Epaminondas music, or see it numbered among his accomplishments, that he danced gracefully, and played skilfully on the flutes 3. But these will be such, for the most part, as, being unacquainted with Greek literature, will think nothing right but what agrees with their own customs.

If these readers will but understand that the same things are not becoming or unbecoming among all people, but that every thing is judged by the usages of men's forefathers, they will not wonder that we, in setting forth the excellencies of the Greeks, have had regard to their manners. For to Cimon, an eminent man among the Athenians, it was thought no disgrace to have his half-sister, 4 by the father's side, in marriage, as his countrymen followed the same practice; but such a union, according to the order of things among us, is deemed unlawful. In Greece it is considered an honour to young men to have as many lovers 5 as possible. At Lacedaemon there is no widow 6 so noble that will not go upon the stage, if engaged for a certain sum. Through the whole of Greece it was accounted a great glory to be proclaimed a conqueror at Olympia; while to appear upon the stage, and become a spectacle to the public,7 was a dishonour to no one in that nation; but all these practices are, with us, deemed partly infamous, partly mean, and at variance with respectability. On the other hand, many things in our habits are decorous, which are by them considered unbecoming; for what Roman is ashamed to bring his wife to a feast, or whose consort does not occupy the best room in the house, and live in the midst of company? But in Greece the case is far otherwise; for a wife is neither admitted to a feast, except among relations, nor does she sit anywhere but in the innermost apartment of the house,8 which is called the gynaeconitis, and into which nobody goes who is not connected with her by near relationship.

But both the size of my intended volume, and my haste to relate what I have undertaken, prevent me from saying more on this point. We will therefore proceed to our subject, and relate in this book the lives of eminent commanders.

I. MILTIADES.

Miltiades leads out a colony to the Chersonese; is mocked by the people of Lemnos, I.----Makes himself master of the Chersonese; takes Lemnos and the Cyclades, II.----Is appointed by Darius, when he was making war on Scythia, to guard the bridge over the Ister; suggests a plan for delivering Greece from the Persians; is opposed by Histiaeus, III.----Exhorts his countrymen to meet Darius in the field, IV.----Defeats Darius before the arrival of the allies, V.----How he is rewarded, VI.----Breaks off the siege of Paros, is condemned, and dies in prison, VII.----True cause of his condemnation. VIII.

I. AT the time when Miltiades, the son of Cimon, an Athenian, was eminent above all his countrymen, both for the antiquity of his family, the glory of his forefathers, and his own good conduct,9 and was of such an age that his fellow citizens might not only hope well of him, but assure themselves that he would be such as they found him when he became known, it chanced that the Athenians wished to send colonists to the Chersonese.10 The number of the party being great, and many applying for a share in the expedition, some chosen from among them were sent to Delphi,11 to consult Apollo what leader they should take in preference to any other; for the Thracians at the time had possession of those parts, with whom they would be obliged to contend in war. The Pythia expressly directed them, when they put the question, to take Miltiades as their commander, as, if they did so, their undertakings would be successful. Upon this answer from the oracle, Miltiades set out for the Chersonese with a fleet, accompanied by a chosen body of men,12 and touched at Lemnos, when, wishing to reduce the people of the island under the power of the Athenians, and requesting the Lemnians to surrender of their own accord, they, in mockery, replied that "they would do so, whenever he, leaving home with a fleet, should reach Lemnos by the aid of the wind Aquilo;" for this wind, rising from the north, is contrary to those setting out from Athens. Miltiades, having no time for delay, directed his course to the quarter to which he was bound, and arrived at the Chersonese.

II. Having there, in a short time, scattered the forces of the barbarians, and made himself master of all the territory that he had desired, he strengthened suitable places with fortresses, 13 settled the multitude, which he had brought with him, in the country, and enriched them by frequent excursions. Nor was he less aided, in this proceeding, by good conduct than by good fortune, for after he had, by the valour of his men, routed the troops of the enemy, he settled affairs with the greatest equity, and resolved upon residing in the country himself. He held, indeed, among the inhabitants, the authority of a king, though he wanted the name; and he did not attain this influence more by his power than by his justice. Nor did he the less, on this account, perform his duty to the Athenians, from whom he had come. From these circumstances it happened that he held his office in perpetuity, not less with the consent of those who had sent him, than of those with whom he had gone thither.

Having settled the affairs of the Chersonese in this manner, he returned to Lemnos, and called on the people to deliver up their city to him according to their promise; for they had said that when he, starting from home, should reach their country by the aid of the north wind, they would surrender themselves; "and he had now a home," he told them, "in the Chersonese." The Carians, who then inhabited Lemnos, though the event had fallen out contrary to their expectation, yet being influenced, not by the words, but by the good fortune of their adversaries, did not venture to resist, but withdrew out of the island. With like success he reduced some other islands, which are called the Cyclades, under the power of the Athenians.

III. About the same period, Darius, king of Persia, resolved upon transporting his army from Asia into Europe, and making war upon the Scythians. He constructed a bridge over the river Ister, by which he might lead across his forces. Of this bridge he left as guardians, during his absence,14 the chiefs 15 whom he had brought with him from Ionia and Aeolia, and to whom he had given the sovereignty of their respective cities; for he thought that he should most easily keep under his power such of the inhabitants of Asia as spoke Greek, if he gave their towns to be held by his friends, to whom, if he should be crushed,16 no hope of safety would be left. Among the number of those, to whom the care of the bridge was then entrusted, was Miltiades.

As several messengers brought word that Darius was unsuccessful in his enterprise, and was hard pressed by the Scythians, Miltiades, in consequence, exhorted the guardians of the bridge not to lose an opportunity, presented them by by fortune, of securing the liberty of Greece; for if Darius should be destroyed, together with the army that he had taken with him, not only Europe would be safe, but also those who, being Greeks by birth, inhabited Asia, would be freed from the dominion of the Persians, and from all danger. "This," he said, "might easily be accomplished, for, if the bridge were broken down, the king would perish in a few days, either by the sword of the enemy, or by famine." After most of them had assented to this proposal, Histiaeus of Miletus, prevented the design from being executed; saying that "the same course would not be expedient for those who held sovereign command, as for the multitude, since their authority depended on the power of Darius, and, if he were cut off, they would be deprived of their governments, and suffer punishment at the hands of their subjects;17 and that he himself, therefore, was so far from agreeing in opinion with the rest, that he thought nothing more advantageous for them than that the kingdom of the Persians should be upheld." As most went over to this opinion, Miltiades, not doubting that his proposal, since so many were acquainted with it, would come to the ears of the king, quitted the Chersonese, and went again to reside at Athens. His suggestion, though it did not take effect, is yet highly to be commended, as he showed himself a greater friend to the general liberty than to his own power.

IV. Darius, when he had returned from Asia into Europe, prepared, at the exhortation of his friends, in order to reduce Greece under his dominion, a fleet of five hundred ships, and appointed Datis and Artaphernes to the command of it, to whom he assigned two hundred thousand infantry and ten thousand cavalry; alleging as a reason for his enterprise, that he was an enemy to the Athenians, because, with their aid, the Ionians had stormed Sardis 18 and put his garrison to death. These generals of the king, having brought up their fleet to Euboea, soon took Eretria, carried off all the citizens of the place,19 and sent them into Asia to the king. They then went to Attica, and drew up their forces in the plain of Marathon, which is distant from the city of Athens about ten miles. The Athenians, though alarmed at this sudden descent, so near and so menacing, sought assistance nowhere but from the Spartans, and despatched Phidippides, a courier of the class called hemerodromoi,20 to Lacedaemon, to acquaint them how speedy assistance they needed. At home, meanwhile, they appointed ten captains to command the army, and among them Miltiades.

Among these captains there was a great discussion, whether they should defend themselves within the walls, or march out to meet the enemy, and decide the contest in the field. Miltiades was the only one extremely urgent that a camp should be formed as soon as possible; "for," he said, "if that were done, not only would courage be added to their countrymen, when they saw that there was no distrust of their valour, but the enemy, from the same cause, would be less bold, if they saw that the Athenians would venture to oppose them with so small a force."

V. In this crisis no state gave assistance to the Athenians, except that of Plataea, which sent them a thousand men. On the arrival of these, the number of ten thousand armed men was made up; a band which was animated with an extraordinary ardour to fight. Hence it happened that Miltiades had more influence than his colleagues, for the Athenians, incited by his authority, led out their forces from the city, and pitched their camp in an eligible place. The next day, having set themselves in array at the foot of the hills opposite the enemy, they engaged in battle with a novel stratagem, and with the utmost impetuosity. For trees had been strewed in many directions, with this intention, that, while they themselves were covered by the high hills,21 the enemy's cavalry might be impeded by the spread of trees, so that they might not be surrounded by numbers. Datis, though he saw that the ground was unfavourable for his men, yet, depending on the number of his force, was desirous to engage, and the rather, because he thought it of advantage to fight before the Spartans came to the enemy's assistance. He led into the field, therefore, a hundred thousand foot and ten thousand horse, and proceeded to battle. In the encounter the Athenians, through their valour, had so much the advantage, that they routed ten times the number of the enemy, and threw them into such a consternation, that the Persians betook themselves, not to their camp, but to their ships. Than this battle there has hitherto been none more glorious; for never did so small a band overthrow so numerous a host.

VI. For this victory it does not seem improper to state what reward was conferred on Miltiades, that it may be the more easily understood that the nature of all states is the same; for as honours among our own people were once few and inexpensive, and for that reason highly prized, but are now costly and common, so we find that it formerly was among the Athenians. For to this very Miltiades, who had saved Athens and the whole of Greece, such honour only was granted, that when the battle of Marathon was painted in the portico called Poecile,22 his figure was placed first in the number of the ten commanders, and he was represented as encouraging his men, and commencing the battle. The same people, after they acquired greater power, and were corrupted by the largesses of their rulers, decreed three hundred statues to Demetrius Phalereus.

VII. After this battle the Athenians gave Miltiades a fleet of seventy ships, that he might make war on the islands that had assisted the barbarians. In the discharge of this commission he obliged most of them to return to their duty; 23 some he took by assault. Being unable to gain over by persuasion one of their number, the island of Paros, which was vain of its strength, he drew his troops out of his ships, invested the town,24 and cut off all their supplies; soon after, he erected his vineae 25 and tortoises, and came close up to the walls. When he was on the point of taking the town, a grove on the main land, which was some distance off, but visible from the island, was set on fire, by I know not what accident, in the night; and when the flame of it was seen by the townsmen and besiegers, it was imagined by both that it was a signal given by the men of the king's fleet; whence it happened that both the Parians were deterred 26 from surrendering, and Miltiades, fearing that the royal fleet was approaching, set fire to the works which he had erected, and returned to Athens with the same number of ships with which he had set out, to the great displeasure of his countrymen. He was in consequence accused of treason, on the allegation, that "when he might have taken Paros, he desisted from the siege, without effecting anything, through being bribed by the king of Persia." He was at this time ill of the wounds which he had received in besieging the town, and, as he could not plead for himself, his brother Tisagoras spoke for him. The cause being heard, he was not condemned to death, but sentenced to pay a fine, which was fixed at fifty talents, a sum equivalent to that which had been spent on the fleet. As he could not pay this money, he was thrown into prison, and there ended his life.

VIII. Although he was brought to trial on the charge relating to Paros, yet there was another cause for his condemnation; for the Athenians, in consequence of the tyranny of Pisistratus, which had occurred a few years before, looked with dread on the aggrandizement of any one of their citizens. Miltiades having been much engaged in military and civil offices, was not thought likely to be contented in a private station, especially as he might seem to be drawn by the force of habit to long for power; for he had held uninterrupted sovereignty in the Chersonesus during all the years that he had dwelt there, and had been called a tyrant, though a just one; for he had not acquired his power by violence, but by the consent of his countrymen, and had maintained his authority by the uprightness of his conduct. But all are esteemed and called tyrants, who become possessed of permanent power in any state which had previously enjoyed liberty. In Miltiades, however, there was both the greatest philanthropy and a wonderful affability, so that there was no person so humble as not to have free access to him; he had also the greatest influence among all the states of Greece, with a noble name, and reputation for military achievements. The people, looking to these circumstances, chose rather that he should suffer, though innocent, than that they should continue longer in fear of him.

II. THEMISTOCLES.

Youth of Themistocles; he is disinherited by his father, I.----His eminence in the Corcyraean and Persian wars, II.----Battle of Artemisium, III.----His stratagem against Xerxes at Salamis, IV.----Causes Xerxes to quit Greece, V.----Builds the walls of Athens, deceiving the Lacedaemonians, VI. VII.----Is ostracised, and seeks refuge in various places, VIII.----His letter to Artaxerxes, and reception by him; dies at Magnesia, IX.

I. THEMISTOCLES was the son of Neocles, an Athenian. The vices of his early youth were compensated by great virtues, so that no one is thought superior, and few are considered equal to him.

But we must begin from the beginning. His father Neocles was of a good family, and married a native of Acharnae,27 of whom Themistocles was the son. Falling under the displeasure of his parents, because he lived too freely, and took no care of his property, he was disinherited by his father. This disgrace, however, did not dishearten him, but incited him to exertion, for being aware that it could not be obliterated without the utmost efforts on his part, he devoted himself wholly to affairs of state, studying diligently to benefit his friends as well as his own reputation. He was much engaged in private causes, and appeared often before the assembly of the people; no matter of importance was managed without him; he quickly discovered what was necessary to be done, and readily explained it in his speeches. Nor was he less ready in managing business than in devising plans for it, for, as Thucydides says, he formed a most accurate judgment of present affairs, and the shrewdest conjectures as to the future. Hence it happened that he soon became distinguished.

II. His first step in the management of public affairs was in the Corcyraean war.28 Being chosen commander by the people to conduct it, he increased the confidence of the citizens, not only as to the struggle in which they were engaged, but for time to come. As the public money, which came in from the mines, was annually wasted by the profusion 29 of the magistrates, he prevailed on the people that a fleet of a hundred ships should be built with that money. This being soon constructed, he first reduced the Corcyraeans, and then, by vigorously pursuing the pirates, rendered the sea secure. In acting thus, he both supplied the Athenians with wealth, and made them extremely skilful in naval warfare. How much this contributed to the safety of Greece in general, was discovered in the Persian war, when Xerxes assailed the whole of Europe by sea and land, with such a force as no man ever had, before or since; for his fleet consisted of two hundred ships of war, on which two thousand transport vessels attended, and his land force was seven hundred thousand foot, and four hundred thousand horse.

When the news of his approach was spread through Greece, and the Athenians, on account of the battle of Marathon, were said to be the chief objects of his attack, they sent to Delphi to ask what they should do in their present circumstances. As soon as they put the question, the Pythian priestess replied that "they must defend themselves with wooden walls." As no one understood to what this answer tended, Themistocles suggested that it was Apollo's recommendation that they should put themselves and their property on board their ships, for that such were the wooden walls intended by the god. This plan being approved, they added to their former vessels as many more with three banks of oars, and carried off all their goods that could be moved, partly to Salamis and partly to Troezen. The citadel, and sacred things, they committed to the priests, and a few old men, to be taken care of; the rest of the town they abandoned.

III. This measure of Themistocles was unsatisfactory to most of the states, and they preferred to fight on land. A select force was accordingly sent with Leonidas, king of the Lacedaemonians, to secure the pass of Thermopylae, and prevent the barbarians from advancing further. This body could not withstand the force of the enemy, and were all slain on the spot. But the combined fleet of Greece, consisting of three hundred ships, of which two hundred belonged to the Athenians, engaged the king's fleet for the first time at Artemisium, between Euboea and the main land; for Themistocles had betaken himself to the straits, that he might not be surrounded by numbers. Though they came off here with success equally balanced, yet they did not dare to remain in the same place, because there was apprehension, lest, if part of the enemy's fleet should get round Euboea, they should be assailed by danger on both sides. Hence it came to past that they left Artemisium, and drew up their fleet on the coast of Salamis, over against Athens.

IV. Xerxes, having forced a passage through Thermopylae marched at once to the city, and as none defended it, destroyed it by fire, putting to death the priests that he found in the citadel.

As those on board the fleet, alarmed at the report of this catastrophe, did not dare to remain where they were, and most of them gave their opinion that they should return to their respective homes, and defend themselves within their walls, Themistocles alone opposed it, saying that united they would be a match for the enemy, but declaring that if they separated they would be destroyed. That this would be the case he assured Eurybiades, king of the Lacedaemonians, who then held the chief command, but making less impression on him than he wished, he sent one of his slaves, the most trustworthy that he had, to Xerxes in the night, to tell him in his own precise words, that "his enemies were retreating, and that, if they should make off, he would require more labour and longer time to finish the war, as he would have to pursue those singly, whom, if he attacked them immediately, he might destroy in a body and at once." The object of this communication was, that all the Greeks should be forced to fight even against their will. The barbarian, receiving this intimation, and not suspecting any guile to be hidden under it, engaged, the day after, in a place most unfavourable for himself, and most advantageous for the enemy, the strait being so confined30 that the body of his fleet could not be brought into action. He was defeated in consequence rather by the stratagem of Themistocles than by the arms of Greece.

V Though Xerxes had thus mismanaged his affairs, he had yet so vast a force left, that even with this he might have overpowered his enemies. But in the meanwhile 31 he was driven from his position by the same leader. For Themistocles, fearing that he would persist in protracting the contest, sent him notice that it was in contemplation that the bridge, which he had made over the Hellespont, should be broken up, and that he should thus be prevented from returning into Asia; and he convinced him that such was the fact. In consequence Xerxes returned into Asia in less than thirty days, by the same way by which he had spent six months in coming, and considered himself not conquered, but saved, by Themistocles. Thus Greece was delivered by the policy of one man, and Asia succumbed to Europe. This is a second victory that may be compared with the triumph at Marathon; for the greatest fleet in the memory of man was conquered in like manner 32 at Salamis by a small number of ships

VI Themistocles was great in this war, and was not less distinguished in peace; for as the Athenians used the harbour of Phalerum, which was neither large nor convenient, the triple port of the Piraeeus 33 was constructed by his advice, and enclosed with walls, so that it equalled the city in magnificence, and excelled it in utility. He also rebuilt the walls of Athens at his own individual risk, for the Lacedaemonians, having found a fair pretext, in consequence of the inroads of the barbarians, for saying that no walled town should be kept up without the Peloponnesus, in order that there might be no fortified places of which the enemy might take possession, attempted to prevent the Athenians from building them. This attempt had a far different object from that which they wished to be apparent; for the Athenians, by their two victories at Marathon and Salamis, had gained so much renown among all people, that the Lacedaemonians became aware that they should have a struggle with them for the supremacy. They therefore wished the Athenians to be as weak as possible.

After they heard, however, that the erection of the wall was begun, they sent ambassadors to Athens to prevent it from being continued. While the ambassadors were present, they desisted, and said that they would send an embassy to them respecting the matter. This embassy Themistocles undertook, and set out first by himself, desiring that the rest of the ambassadors should follow when the height of the wall should seem sufficiently advanced; and that, in the meantime, all the people, slaves as well as freemen, should carry on the work, sparing no place, whether sacred or profane, public or private, but collecting from all quarters whatever they thought suitable for building. Hence it happened that the walls of the Athenians were constructed of materials from temples and tombs.

VII. Themistocles, when he arrived at Lacedaemon, would not go to the authorities at once, but endeavoured to make as much delay as possible, alleging, as a reason, that he was waiting for his colleagues. While the Lacedaemonians were complaining that the work was nevertheless continued, and that he was trying to deceive them in the matter, the rest of the ambassadors in the meantime arrived; and, as he learned from them that but little of the wall remained to be done, he proceeded to the Lacedaemonian Ephori, in whom the supreme power was vested, and assured them positively that "false accounts had been given them," adding "that it would be proper for them to send persons of character and respectability, in whom trust might be placed, to inquire into the affair; and that in the meantime they might detain himself as a hostage.' His suggestion was complied with, and three deputies, men who had filled the highest offices, were despatched to Athens.

When Themistocles thought that they had reached the city, he went to the Ephori and senate of the Lacedaemonians, and boldly stated that "the Athenians, by his advice, had enclosed their public gods, and their national and household gods,[34] with walls, that they might more easily defend them from the enemy, a step which they were at liberty to take by the common law of nations; nor had they, in acting thus, done what was useless to Greece; for their city stood as a bulwark against the barbarians, at which the king's fleets had already twice suffered shipwreck; and that the Lacedaemonians acted unreasonably and unjustly, in regarding rather what was conducive to their own dominion, than what would be of advantage to the whole of Greece. If, therefore, they wished to receive back the deputies whom they had sent to Athens, they must permit him to return; otherwise they would never receive them into their country again."

VIII. Yet he did not escape jealousy on the part of his own countrymen; for being expelled from the city by the ostracism, through the same apprehension from which Miltiades had been condemned, he went to dwell at Argos. While he was living there in great honour, on account of his many excellent qualities, the Lacedaemonians sent ambassadors to Athens to accuse him in his absence of having made a league with the king of Persia to subjugate Greece. On this charge he was condemned, while absent, of treason to his country. As soon as he heard of this sentence, he removed, as he did not think himself safe at Argos, to Corcyra. But perceiving that the leading men of that state were afraid lest the Lacedaemonians and Athenians should declare war against them on his account, he fled to Admetus, king of the Molossi, with whom he had had a great friendship. [35] Having arrived here, and the king being absent at the time, he, in order that he might secure himself, if received, with the stronger safeguard of religion, took up the king's little daughter, and ran with her into a certain temple, which was regarded with the utmost veneration, and from which he did not come out till the king having given him his right hand, took him under his protection; an engagement which he strictly observed. For when his surrender was publicly demanded by the Athenians and Lacedaemonians, he did not betray his dependant, but warned him to consult for his safety, as it would be difficult for him to live in security in a place so near to Greece. He in consequence caused him to be conducted to Pydna, appointing him a sufficient guard. Here he went on board a ship, to all the sailors in which he was personally unknown. The vessel being driven by a violent storm towards Naxos, where the army of the Athenians then lay, Themistocles felt assured that, if he put in there, he must lose his life. Being thus compelled by necessity, he disclosed to the captain of the ship who he was, promising him a large reward if he would save him. The captain, moved with concern for so illustrious a man, kept the ship at anchor in the open sea, at some distance from the island, for a day and a night, allowing no person to quit it. Thence he went to Ephesus, where he set Themistocles on shore, who afterwards liberally rewarded him for his services.

IX. I know most historians have related that Themistocles went over into Asia in the reign of Xerxes, but I give credence to Thucydides in preference to others, because he, of all who have left records of that period, was nearest in point of time to Themistocles, and was of the same city. Thucydides says that he went to Artaxerxes, and sent him a letter in these words: "I, Themistocles, am come to you, a man, who, of all the Greeks, brought most evil upon your house, when I was obliged to war against your father, and to defend my own country. I also did your father still greater service, after I myself was in safety, and he began to be in danger; for when he wished, after the battle fought at Salamis, to return into Asia, I informed him by letter that it was in contemplation that the bridge, which he had constructed over the Hellespont, should be broken up, and that he should be surrounded by enemies; by which information he was rescued from danger. But now, pursued by all Greece, I have fled to you, soliciting your favour, and if I shall obtain it, you will find me no less deserving as a friend than your father found me resolute as an enemy. I make this request, however, that with regard to the subjects on which I wish to discourse with you, you would grant me a year's delay, and when that time is past, permit me to approach you."

X. The king, admiring his greatness of mind, and wishing to have such a man attached to him, granted his request. Themistocles devoted all that time to the writings and language of the Persians, in which he acquired such knowledge, that he is said to have spoken before the king with much more propriety 36 than those could who were born in Persia. After he had made the king many promises, and what was most agreeable of them all, that if he would follow his advice, he might conquer Greece in war, he was honoured with rich presents by Artaxerxes, and returning into Asia Minor, fixed his habitation at Magnesia. For the king had bestowed upon him this city, expressing himself in these words, that "it was to supply him with bread;" (from the land about this place fifty talents came into him annually;) and he had also given him Lampsacus, "whence he might get his wine," and Myus, "from which he might have meats for his table."37

Two memorials of Themistocles have remained to our times; his sepulchre near the city,38 in which he was buried, and his statues in the forum of Magnesia. Concerning his death various accounts have been given by several writers; we prefer, to all others, the authority of Thucydides, who says that he died of some disease at Magnesia, though he admits that there was a report that he voluntarily took poison, because he despaired of being able to perform what he had promised the king about subjugating Greece. Thucydides has also recorded that his bones were buried by his friends in Attica privately, it not being permitted by law to bury them, as he had been pronounced guilty of treason.

III. ARISTIDES.

Aristides the contemporary and rival of Themistocles; is banished, I. ----After his recall, commands against Mardonius; increases the popularity of the Athenians, II.----Has the care of the treasury, dies poor, III.

I. ARISTIDES, the son of Lysimachus, a native of Athens, was almost of the same age with Themistocles, and contended with him, in consequence, for pre-eminence, as they were determined rivals one to the other; 39 and it was seen in their case how much eloquence could prevail over integrity; for though Aristides was so distinguished for uprightness of conduct,40 that he was the only person in the memory of man (as far at least as I have heard) who was called by the surname of JUST, yet being overborne by Themistocles with the ostracism, he was condemned to be banished for ten years.

Aristides, finding that the excited multitude could not be appeased, and noticing, as he yielded to their violence, a person writing that he ought to be banished, is said to have asked him "why he did so, or what Aristides had done, that he should be thought deserving of such a punishment?" The person writing replied, that "he did not know Aristides, but that he was not pleased that he had laboured to be called Just beyond other men."

He did not suffer the full sentence of ten years appointed by law, for when Xerxes made a descent upon Greece, he was recalled into his country by a decree of the people, about six years after he had been exiled.

II. He was present, however, in the sea-fight at Salamis, which was fought before he was allowed to return. 41 He was also commander of the Athenians at Plataeae, in the battle in which Mardonius was routed, and the army of the barbarians was cut off. Nor is there any other celebrated act of his in military affairs recorded, besides the account of this command; but of his justice, equity, and self-control, there are many instances. Above all, it was through his integrity, when he was joined in command of the common fleet of Greece with Pausanias, under whose leadership Mardonius had been put to flight, that the supreme authority at sea was transferred from the Lacedaemonians to the Athenians; for before that time the Lacedaemonians had the command both by sea and land. But at this period it happened, through the indiscreet conduct of Pausanias, and the equity of Aristides, that all the states of Greece attached themselves as allies to the Athenians, and chose them as their leaders against the barbarians.

III. 42 In order that they might repel the barbarians more easily, if perchance they should try to renew the war, Aristides was chosen to settle what sum of money each state should contribute for building fleets and equipping troops. By his appointment four hundred and sixty talents were deposited annually at Delos, which they fixed upon to be the common treasury; but all this money was afterwards removed to Athens.

How great was his integrity, there is no more certain proof, than that, though he had been at the head of such important affairs, he died in such poverty that he scarcely left money to defray the charges of his funeral. Hence it was that his daughters were brought up at the expense of the country, and were married with dowries given them from the public treasury. He died about four years after Themistocles was banished from Athens.

IV. PAUSANIAS

Pausanias at Plataeae, I.----He takes Byzantium, and makes advances to Xerxes, II.----His conduct abroad; his imprisonment, III.---- He betrays his guilt, IV.----His death at the temple of Minerva, V.

I. PAUSANIAS the Lacedaemonian was a great man, but of varied character in all the relations of life; for as he was ennobled by virtues, he was also obscured by vices. His most famous battle was that at Plataeae, for, under his command Mardonius, a royal satrap, by birth a Mede, and son-in-law to the king (a man, among the chief of all the Persians, brave in action and full of sagacity), at the head of two hundred thousand infantry, whom he had chosen man by man, and twenty thousand cavalry, was routed by no very large army of Greeks; and the general himself was slain in the struggle.

Elated by this victory, he began to indulge in irregular proceedings,43 and to covet greater power. But he first incurred blame on this account, that he offered at Delphi, out of the spoil, a golden tripod with an inscription written upon it, in which was this statement, that "the barbarians had been cut off at Plataeae by his management, and that, on account of that victory, he had presented this offering to Apollo." These lines the Lacedaemonians erased, and wrote nothing but the names of the states by whose aid the Persians had been conquered.

II. After this battle they sent Pausanias with the confederate fleet to Cyprus and the Hellespont, to expel the garrisons of the barbarians from those parts. Experiencing equal good fortune in this enterprise, he began to conduct himself still more haughtily, and to aim at still higher matters; for having, at the taking of Byzantium, captured several Persian noblemen, and among them some relations of the king, he sent them secretly back to Xerxes, and pretended that they had escaped out of prison. He sent with them, also, Gongylus of Eretria, to carry a letter to the king, in which Thucydides 44 has recorded that the following words were written:

"Pausanias, the general of Sparta, having discovered that those whom he took at Byzantium are your relations, has sent them back as a gift, and desires to be joined in affinity with you. If therefore it seem good to you, give him your daughter in marriage. Should you do so, he engages, with your aid, to bring both Sparta and the rest of Greece under your sway. If you wish anything to be done with regard to these proposals, be careful to send a trustworthy person to him, with whom he may confer."

The king, extremely delighted at the restoration of so many persons so nearly related to him, immediately despatched Artabazus with a letter to Pausanias, in which he commended him, and begged that he would spare no pains to accomplish what he promised; if he effected it, he should never meet with a refusal of anything from him. Pausanias, learning what the king's pleasure was, and growing more eager for the accomplishment of his designs, fell under the suspicion of the Lacedaemonians. In the midst of his proceedings, accordingly, he was recalled home, and being brought to trial on a capital charge, was acquitted on it, but sentenced to pay a fine; for which reason he was not sent back to the fleet.

III. Not long after, however, he returned to the army of his own accord, and there, not in a sensible, but in an insane manner, let his views become known; for he laid aside, not only the manners of his country, but its fashions and dress. He adopted regal splendour and Median attire; Median and Egyptian guards attended him; he had his table served, after the Persian manner, more luxuriously than those who were with him could endure; he refused permission to approach him to those who sought it; he gave haughty replies and severe commands. To Sparta he would not return, but withdrew to Colonae, a place in the country of Troas, where he formed designs pernicious both to his country and himself. When the Lacedaemonians knew of his proceedings, they sent deputies to him with a scytala,[45] on which it was written, after their fashion,[46] that "if he did not return home, they would condemn him to death." Being alarmed at this communication, but hoping that he should be able, by his money and his influence, to ward off the danger that threatened him, he returned home. As soon as he arrived there, he was thrown into the public prison by the Ephori, for it is allowable, by their laws, for any one of the Ephori to do this to a king.[47] He however got himself freed from confinement, but was not cleared from suspicion, for the belief still prevailed, that he had made a compact with the king of Persia.

There is a certain class of men called Helots, of whom a great number till the lands of the Lacedaemonians, and perform the duties of slaves. These men he was thought to have solicited, by holding out to them hopes of liberty, to join him. But as there was no visible ground for a charge against him on these points, on which he might be convicted, they did not think that they ought to pronounce, concerning so eminent and famous a man, on suspicion only, but that they must wait till the affair should disclose itself.

IV. In the meantime a certain Argilian,[48] a young man whom, in his boyhood, Pausanias had loved with an ardent affection,[49] having received a letter from him for Artabazus, and conceiving a suspicion that there was something written in it about himself, because no one of those who had been sent to the same place on such an errand, had returned, loosed the string of the letter,50 and taking off the seal, discovered that if he delivered it he would lose his life. In the letter were also some particulars respecting matters that had been arranged between the king and Pausanias. This letter he delivered to the Ephori. The cautious prudence of the Lacedaemonians, on this occasion, is not to be passed without notice; for they were not induced, even by this man's information, to seize Pausanias, nor did they think that violent measures should be adopted, until he gave proof of his own guilt.

They accordingly directed the informer what they wished to have done. At Taenarus there is a temple of Neptune, which the Greeks account it a heinous crime to profane. To this temple the informer fled, and sat down on the steps of the altar. Close to the building, they made a recess underground, from which, if any one held communication with the Argilian, he might be overheard; and into this place some of the Ephori went down. Pausanias, when he heard that the Argilian had fled to the altar, came thither in great trepidation, and seeing him sitting as a suppliant at the altar of the divinity, he inquired of him what was the cause of so sudden a proceeding. The Argilian then informed him what he had learned from the letter, and Pausanias being so much the more agitated, began to entreat him "not to make any discovery, or to betray him who deserved great good at his hands;" adding that, "if he would but grant him this favour, and assist him when involved in such perplexities, it should be of great advantage to him

V. The Ephori, hearing these particulars, thought it better that he should be apprehended in the city. After they had set out thither, and Pausanias, having, as he thought, pacified the Argilian, was also returning to Lacedaemon, he understood (just as he was on the point of being made prisoner) by a look from one of the Ephori who wished to warn him, that some secret mischief was intended against him. He accordingly fled for refuge, a few steps before those who pursued him, into the temple of Minerva, which is called Chalcioecos.51 That he might not escape from thence, the Ephori immediately blocked up the folding-doors of the temple, and pulled off the roof, that he might more readily die in the open air. It is said that the mother of Pausanias was then living, and that, though very aged, she was among the first to bring a stone, when she heard of her son's guilt, to the door of the temple, in order to shut him in. Thus Pausanias tarnished his great glory in war by a dishonourable death.

As soon as he was carried, half-dead, out of the temple, he gave up the ghost. When some said that his body ought to be carried to the place where those given up to capital punishment were buried, the proposal was displeasing to the majority, and they interred him at some distance from the spot in which he died. He was afterwards removed from thence, in consequence of an admonition from the Delphic god, and buried in the same place where he had ended his life.

V. CIMON.

Cimon is compelled to go to prison on the death of his father; is liberated by his wife, I.-----
His character and actions; he defeats the Persians by land and sea on the same day, II.----Is

ostracised and recalled, and makes peace with the Lacedaemonians; his death, III.----His praises, IV.

I. CIMON, the son of Miltiades, an Athenian, experienced a very unhappy entrance on manhood; for as his father had been unable to pay to the people the fine imposed upon him, and had consequently died in the public gaol, Cimon was kept in prison, nor could he, by the Athenian laws,52 be set at liberty, unless he paid the sum of money that his father had been fined. He had married, however, his sister by the father's side,53 named Elpinice, induced not more by love than by custom; for the Athenians are allowed to marry their sisters by the same father; and a certain Callias, a man whose birth was not equal to his wealth, and who had made a great fortune from the mines, being desirous of having her for a wife, tried to prevail on Cimon to resign her to him, saying that if he obtained his desire, he would pay the fine for him. Though Cimon received such a proposal with scorn, Elpinice said that she would not allow a son of Miltiades to die in the public prison, when she could prevent it; and that she would marry Callias if he would perform what he promised.

II. Cimon, being thus set free from confinement, soon attained great eminence; for he had considerable eloquence, the utmost generosity, and great skill, not only in civil law, but in military affairs, as he had been employed from his boyhood with his father in the army. He in consequence held the people of the city under his control, and had great influence over the troops. In his first term of service, on the river Strymon, he put to flight great forces of the Thracians, founded the city of Amphipolis, and sent thither ten thousand Athenian citizens as a colony. He also, in a second expedition, conquered and took at Mycale a fleet of two hundred ships belonging to the Cyprians and Phoenicians, and experienced like good fortune by land on the same day; for after capturing the enemy's vessels, he immediately led out his troops from the fleet, and overthrew at the first onset a vast force of the barbarians. By this victory he obtained a great quantity of spoil; and, as some of the islands, through the rigour of the Athenian government, had revolted from them, he secured the attachment, in the course of his return home, of such as were well disposed, and obliged the disaffected to return to their allegiance. Scyros, which the Dolopes at that time inhabited, he depopulated, because it had behaved itself insolently, ejecting the old settlers from the city and island, and dividing the lands among his own countrymen. The Thasians, who relied upon their wealth, he reduced as soon as he attacked them. With these spoils the citadel of Athens was adorned on the side which looks to the south.

III. When, by these acts, he had attained greater honour in the state than any other man, he fell under the same public odium as his father, and others eminent among the Athenians; for by the votes of the shells, which they call the ostracism, he was condemned to ten years' exile. Of this proceeding the Athenians repented sooner than himself; for after he had submitted, with great fortitude, to the ill-feeling of his ungrateful countrymen, and the Lacedaemonians had declared war against the Athenians, a desire for his well-known bravery immediately ensued. In consequence, he was summoned back to his country five years after he had been banished from it. But as he enjoyed the guest-friendship 54 of the Lacedaemonians, he thought it better to hasten to Sparta, and accordingly proceeded thither of his own accord, and settled a peace between those two most powerful states.

Being sent as commander, not long after, to Cyprus, with a fleet of two hundred ships, he fell sick, after he had conquered the greater part of the island, and died in the town of Citium.

IV. The Athenians long felt regret for him, not only in war, but in time of peace; for he was a man of such liberality, that though he had farms and gardens in several parts, he never set a guard over them for the sake of preserving the fruit, so that none might be hindered from enjoying his property as he pleased. Attendants always followed him with money, that, if any one asked his assistance, he might have something to give him immediately, lest, by putting him off, he should appear to refuse. Frequently, when he saw a man thrown in his way by chance 55 in a shabby dress, he gave him his own cloak. A dinner was dressed for him daily in such abundance, that he could invite all whom he saw in the forum uninvited; a ceremony which he did not fail to observe every day. His protection, his assistance, his pecuniary means, were withheld from none. He enriched many; and he buried at his own cost many poor persons, who at their death had not left sufficient for their interment. In consequence of such conduct, it is not at all surprising that his life was free from trouble, and his death severely felt.

VI. LYSANDER.

Lysander conquers the Athenians, and establishes a decemvirate in the several states of Greece, I ----His cruelty to the Thracians, II.----He endeavours to dethrone the kings of Sparta, and corrupt the various oracles; is brought to trial and acquitted; is killed by the Thebans, III.----Was his own accuser, IV.

I. LYSANDER, the Lacedaemonian, left a high character of himself, which was gained, however, more by good fortune than by merit. That he subdued the Athenians, when they were at war with the Lacedaemonians, in the twenty-sixth year of the contest, is certain; but how he obtained that conquest is but little known; for it was not effected by the valour of his own troops, but by the want of discipline among the enemy, who, from not being obedient to the commands of their leaders, but straggling about in the fields, and abandoning their vessels, fell into the power of their adversaries; in consequence of which disaster the Athenians submitted to the Lacedaemonians.

Lysander, elated with this victory, and having always before been a factious and bold man, allowed himself such liberty, that the Lacedaemonians, through his conduct, incurred the greatest unpopularity throughout Greece; for they having said that their object in going to war was to humble the overbearing tyranny of the Athenians, Lysander, after he had captured the enemy's fleet at Aegospotamos, endeavoured after nothing so much as to keep all the states of Greece under his authority, while he pretended that he acted thus for the sake of the Lacedaemonians. Having every where ejected those who favoured the party of the Athenians, he made choice of ten men in each city, on whom he conferred supreme authority, and the control of all proceedings. Into the number of these no one was admitted who was not attached to him by friendship, or who had not assured him, by pledging his faith, that he would be entirely at his disposal.

II. The decemviral government being thus established in every city, everything was done according to his pleasure. Of his cruelty and perfidy it is sufficient to give one instance, by way of example, that we may not weary our readers by enumerating many acts of the same individual. As he was returning in triumph from Asia, and had turned aside towards Thasos, he endeavoured, as the people had been eminent for fidelity to the Athenians, to corrupt them,56 as if those were wont to be the firmest friends who had been steady enemies. But he saw that unless he concealed his intention in the affair, the Thasians would elude him, and take measures for their own interests. Accordingly 57 ....

III. The decemviral government, which had been appointed by him, his countrymen abolished. Incensed at this affront, he entered upon measures to remove the kings of the Lacedaemonians; but he found that he could not effect his object without support from the gods, because the Lacedaemonians were accustomed to refer everything to the oracles. In the first place, therefore, he endeavoured to corrupt Delphi, and, when he could not succeed in doing so, he made an attempt upon Dodona. Being disappointed there also, he gave out that he had made vows which he must pay to Jupiter Ammon, thinking that he would bribe the Africans with greater ease. When he had gone, accordingly, with this expectation into Africa, the priests of Jupiter greatly disappointed him, for they not only would not be bribed, but even sent deputies to Lacedaemon to accuse Lysander of "having endeavoured to corrupt the ministers of the temple." After being brought to trial on this charge, and being acquitted by the votes of his judges, he was sent with some auxiliary troops to the Orchomenians, and killed by the Thebans at Haliartus. How just was the decision regarding him,58 the speech was a proof, which was found in his house after his death, and in which he recommended to the Lacedaemonians, that, after they had abolished the regal government, a leader should be chosen from among the whole people to conduct the war; but it was written in such a manner, that it might seem to be in accordance with the advice of the gods, which he, relying on his money, did not doubt that he should procure. This speech Cleon of Halicarnassus is said to have written for him

IV. In this place a transaction of Pharnabazus, the king's satrap, must not be omitted. When Lysander, as commander of the fleet, had done many cruel and avaricious acts in the course of the war, and suspected that reports of these proceedings had been made to his countrymen, he asked Pharnabazus to give him a testimonial to present to the Ephori, showing with what conscientiousnes he had carried on the war and treated the allies, begging him to write fully concerning the matter, as his authority on that head would be great. Pharnabazus promised him fairly, and wrote a long and full letter,59 in which he extolled him with the greatest praises. But when Lysander had read and approved of it, Pharnabazus substituted, while it was being sealed, another of the same size in its place, so like it that it could not be distinguished from it, in which he had most circumstantially accused him of avarice and perfidy. Lysander, accordingly, when he had returned home, and had said what he wished before the chief magistrates, handed them, as a testimonial, the letter which he had received from Pharnabazus.

The Ephori, after having perused it when Lysander was withdrawn, gave it to him to read. Thus he became unawares his own accuser.

VII. ALCIBIADES.

Alcibiades eminent both in his virtues and vices, I.----His education, II.----He commands in the expedition against Syracuse; is suspected of profaning the mysteries, and of conspiring against the government, III.----Is recalled home, but flees, and attaches himself to the Lacedaemonians, IV.----Falling under suspicion among them, he flees to the Persians, and is afterwards reconciled to his countrymen, V.----His enthusiastic reception at Athens, VI. ----He again becomes unpopular there; his successes in Thrace, VII.----He tries to promote the good of his country, VIII.----He crosses over into Asia, IX.----Is killed in Phrygia, X.----His character, XI.

I. ALCIBIADES. the son of Clinias, was a native of Athens. In him nature seems to have tried what she could do; for it is agreed among all who have written concerning him, that no one was ever more remarkable than he, either for vices or virtues. Born in a most distinguished city, of a very high family, and by far the most handsome of all the men. of his age, he was qualified for any occupation, and abounded in practical intelligence. He was eminent as a commander by sea and land; he was eloquent, so as to produce the greatest effect by his speeches; for such indeed was the persuasiveness of his looks and language, that in oratory no one was a match for him. He was rich,60 and, when occasion required, laborious, patient, liberal, and splendid, no less in his public than in his private life;61 he was also affable and courteous, conforming dexterously to circumstances; but, when he had unbent himself, and no reason offered why he should endure the labour of thought, was seen to be luxurious, dissolute, voluptuous, and self-indulgent, so that all wondered there should be such dissimilitude, and so contradictory a nature, in the same man.

II. He was brought up in the house of Pericles (for he is said to have been his step-son),62 and was. taught by Socrates. For his father-in-law he had Hipponicus, the richest man of all that spoke the Greek language; so that, even if he had contrived for himself, he could neither have thought of more advantages, nor have secured greater, than those which fortune or nature had bestowed upon him. At his entrance on manhood he was beloved by many, after the manner of the Greeks, and among them by Socrates, whom Plato mentions in his Symposium; for he introduces Alcibiades, saying that "he had passed the night with Socrates, and had not risen up from him otherwise than a son should rise from a father." When he was of maturer age, he had himself no fewer objects of affection, his intercourse with whom, as far as was possible, he did many acts of an objectionable character, in a delicate and agreeable manner; which acts we would relate, had we not other things to tell of a higher and better nature.

III. In the Peloponnesian war, the Athenians, by his advice and persuasion, declared war against the Syracusans, to conduct which he himself was chosen general. Two colleagues were besides assigned him, Nicias and Lamachus. While the expedition was in preparation, and before the fleet sailed, it happened one night that all the statues of Mercury 63 that were in the city of Athens were thrown down, except one, which was before the gate of Andocides, and which, in consequence, was afterwards generally called the Mercury of Andocides.64 As it appeared that this could not have been done without a strong confederacy of many persons, since it had respect not to a private but to a public matter,65 great dread was excited among the multitude, lest some sudden tumult should arise in the city to destroy the people's liberty. The suspicion of this seemed chiefly to attach to Alcibiades, because he was considered both more influential, and of higher standing, than any private person; for he had secured many adherents by his generosity, and had made still more his friends by assisting them in legal proceedings. Hence it happened, that as often as he appeared in public, he drew the eyes of all people upon him; nor was any man in the whole city thought equal to him. They accordingly had not only the greatest hope of him, but also the greatest fear, because he was able to do much harm as well as much good. He was sullied also by ill report, for it was said that he celebrated the mysteries 66 in his own house, a practice which, according to public opinion among the Athenians, was regarded as impious; and this matter was thought to have reference, not to religion, but to a conspiracy.67

IV. Of this crime he was accused by his enemies in a public assembly of the people. But the time for him to set out to the war was drawing near; and he considering this, and being aware of the habit 68 of his countrymen, requested that, if they wished anything to be done concerning him, an examination should rather be held upon him while he was pre sent, than that he should be accused in his absence of a crime against which there was a strong public feeling.69 But his enemies resolved to continue quiet for the present, because they were aware that no hurt could then be done him, and to wait for the time when he should have gone abroad, that they might thus attack him while he was absent. They accordingly did so; for after they supposed that he had reached Sicily, they impeached him, during his absence, of having profaned the sacred rites. In consequence of this affair, a messenger, to desire him to return home to plead his cause, being despatched into Sicily to him by the government, at a time when he had great hopes of managing his province successfully, he yet did not refuse to obey, but went on board a trireme which had been sent to convey him. Arriving in this vessel at Thurii in Italy, and reflecting much with himself on the ungovernable license 70 of his countrymen, and their violent feelings towards the aristocracy, and deeming it most advantageous to avoid the impending storm, he secretly withdrew from his guards, and went from thence first to Elis, and afterwards to Thebes. But when he heard that he was condemned to death, his property having been confiscated, and as had been usual, that the priests called Eumolpidae had been obliged by the people to curse him, and that a copy of the curse, engraven on a stone pillar, had been set up in a public place, in order that the memory of it might be better attested, he removed to Lacedaemon. There, as he was accustomed to declare, he carried on a war, not against his country, but against his enemies, because the same persons were enemies to their own city; for though they knew that he could be of the greatest service to the republic, they had expelled him from it, and consulted their own animosity more than the common advantage. By his advice, in consequence, the Lacedaemonians made an alliance with the king of Persia, and afterwards fortified Deceleia in Attica, and having placed a constant garrison there, kept Athens in a state of blockade. By his means, also, they detached Ionia from its alliance with the Athenians, and after this was done, they began to have greatly the advantage in the contest.

V. Yet by these proceedings they were not so much rendered friends to Alcibiades, as alienated from him by fear; for when they saw the singular intelligence of this most active-minded man in every way, they were afraid that, being moved by love for his country, he might at some time revolt from them, and return into favour with his countrymen. They therefore determined to seek an opportunity for killing him. But this determination could not long be concealed from Alcibiades; for he was a man of such sagacity that he could not be deceived, especially when he turned his attention to putting himself on his guard. He in consequence betook himself to Tissaphernes, a satrap of King Darius; and having gained a way to an intimate friendship with him, and seeing that the power of the Athenians, from the ill success of their attempts in Sicily, was on the decline, while that of the Lacedaemonians, on the other hand, was increasing, he first of all conferred, through messengers, with Pisander the Athenian commander, who had a force at Samos, and made some mention concerning his return; for Pisander, with the same feelings as Alcibiades, was no friend to the power of the people, but a favourer of the aristocracy. Though deserted by him,71 he was received at first, through the agency of Thrasybulus the son of Lycus, by the army, and made commander at Samos; and afterwards, from Theramenes making interest for him, he was recalled by a decree of the people, and, while still absent, was appointed to equal command with Thrasybulus and Theramenes. Under the influence of these leaders, so great a change in affairs took place, that the Lacedaemonians, who had just before flourished as conquerors, were struck with fear and sued for peace; for they had been defeated in five battles by land, and three by sea, in which they had lost two hundred triremes, that had been captured and had fallen into the possession of their enemies. Alcibiades, with his colleagues, had recovered Ionia, the Hellespont, and many Greek cities besides, situated on the coast of Asia, of which they had taken several by storm, and among them Byzantium. Nor had they attached fewer to their interest by policy, as they had exercised clemency towards those who were taken prisoners; and then, laden with spoil, and having enriched the troops and achieved very great exploits, they returned to Athens.

VI. The whole city having gone down to the Piraeeus to meet them, there was such a longing among them all to see Alcibiades, that the multitude flocked to his galley as if he had come alone; for the people were fully persuaded of this, that both their former ill success, and their present good fortune, had happened through his means. They therefore attributed the loss of Sicily, and the victories of the Lacedemonians, to their own fault, in having banished such a man from the country. Nor did they seem to entertain this opinion without reason; for after Alcibiades had begun to command the army, the enemies could withstand them neither by land nor by sea. As soon as he came out of his ship, though Theramenes and Thrasybulus had commanded in the same enterprises, and came into the Piraeeus at the same time with him, yet the people all followed him alone, and (what had never happened before, except in the case of conquerors at Olympia) he was publicly presented with golden and brazen crowns. Such kindness from his countrymen he received with tears, remembering their severity in past times. When he arrived at the city, and an assembly of the people had been called, he addressed them in such a manner, that no one was so unfeeling as not to lament his ill-treatment, and declare himself an enemy to those by whose agency he had been driven from his country, just as if some other people, and not the same people that was then weeping, had sentenced him to suffer for sacrilege. His property was in consequence good to him at the public cost, and the same priests, the Eumolpidae, who had cursed him, were obliged to recall their curses; and the pillars, on which the curse had been written, were thrown into the sea.

VII. This happiness of Alcibiades proved by no means lasting; for after all manner of honours had been decreed him, and the whole management of the state, both at home and in the field, had been committed to him, to be regulated at his sole pleasure, and he had requested that two colleagues, Thrasybulus and Adimantus, should be assigned him (a request which was not refused), proceeding with the fleet to Asia, he fell again under the displeasure of his countrymen, because he did not manage affairs at Cyme 72 to their wish; for they thought that he could do every thing. Hence it happened that they imputed whatever was done unsuccessfully to his misconduct, saying that he acted either carelessly or treacherously, as it fell out on this occasion, for they alleged that he would not take Cyme, because he had been bribed by the king. We consider, therefore, that their extravagant opinion of his abilities and valour was his chief misfortune; since he was dreaded no less than he was loved, lest, elated by good fortune and great power, he should conceive a desire to become a tyrant. From these feelings it resulted, that they took his commission from him in his absence, and put another commander in his place. When he heard of this proceeding, he would not return home, but betook himself to Pactye,73 and there established three fortresses, Borni, Bisanthe, and Neontichos, and having collected a body of troops, was the first man of any Grecian state 74 that penetrated into Thrace, thinking it more glorious to enrich himself with spoils from barbarians than from Greeks. In consequence his fame increased with his power, and he secured to himself a strong alliance with some of the kings of Thrace.

VIII. Yet he could not give up his affection for his country; for when Philocles, the commander of the Athenians, had stationed his fleet at Aegospotamos, and Lysander, the captain of the Lacedaemonians (who was intent upon protracting the war as long as possible, because money was supplied to the Lacedaemonians by the king, while to the exhausted Athenians, on the other hand, nothing was left but their arms and their ships) was not far distant, Alcibiades came to the army of the Athenians, and there, in the presence of the common soldiers, began to assert,75 that "if they pleased, he would force Lysander either to fight or beg peace; that the Lacedaemonians were unwilling to engage by sea, because they were stronger in land-forces than in ships; but that it would be easy for him to bring down Seuthes, king of the Thracians, to drive them from the land, and that, when this was done, they would of necessity either come to an engagement with their fleet, or put an end to the war." Philocles, though he saw that this statement was true, would not yet do what was desired, for he knew that he himself, if Alcibiades were restored to the command, would be of no account with the army; and that, if any success resulted, his share in the matter would amount to nothing, while, on the other hand, if any ill-fortune occurred, he alone would be called to account for the miscarriage. Alcibiades, on taking leave of him, said, "As you hinder your country's success, I advise you to keep your sailors' camp near the enemy; for there is danger that, through the insubordination of our men, an opportunity may be afforded to Lysander of cutting off our army." Nor did his apprehension deceive him; for Lysander, having learned from his scouts that the body of the Athenian force was gone on shore to seek for plunder, and that the ships were left almost empty, did not neglect the opportunity of making an attack, and by that single effort put an end to the whole war.

IX. Alcibiades, after the Athenians were defeated, not thinking those parts sufficiently safe for him, concealed himself in the inland parts of Thrace above the Propontis, trusting that his wealth would most easily escape notice there, But he was disappointed; for the Thracians, when they learned that he had come with a great sum of money, formed a plot against him, and robbed him of what he had brought, but were unable to secure his person. Perceiving that no place was safe for him in Greece, on account of the power of the Lacedemonians, he went over into Asia to Pharnabazus, whom he so charmed, indeed, by his courtesy, that no man had a higher place in his favour; for he gave him Grunium, a strong-hold in Phrygia, from which he annually received fifty talents' revenue.

But with this good fortune Alcibiades was not content, nor could endure that Athens, conquered as she was, should continue subject to the Lacedaemonians. He was accordingly bent, with his whole force of thought, on delivering his country, but saw that that object could not be effected without the aid of the king of Persia, and therefore desired that he should be attached to him as a friend; nor did he doubt that he should easily accomplish his wish, if he had but an opportunity for an interview with him; for he knew that his brother Cyrus was secretly preparing war against him, with the aid of the Lacedaemonians, and foresaw that, if he gave him information of this design, he would find great favour at his hands.

X. While he was trying to effect this object, and entreating Pharnabazus that he might be sent to the king, Critias, and the other tyrants of the Athenians, despatched at the same time persons in their confidence into Asia to Lysander, to acquaint him, that, "unless he cut off Alcibiades, none of those arrangements which he had made at Athens would stand; and therefore, if he wished his acts to remain unaltered, he must pursue him to death." The Lacedaemonian, roused by this message, concluded that he must act in a more decided manner with Pharnabazus. He therefore announced to him, that "the relations which the king had formed with the Lacedaemonians would be of no effect, unless he delivered up Alcibiades alive or dead." The satrap could not withstand this menace, and chose rather to violate the claims of humanity than that the king's interest should suffer. He accordingly sent Sysamithres and Bagaeus to kill Alcibiades, while he was still in Phrygia, and preparing for his journey to the king. The persons sent gave secret orders to the neighbourhood, in which Alcibiades then was, to put him to death. They, not daring to attack him with the sword, collected wood during the night round the cottage in which he was sleeping, and set light to it, that they might despatch by fire him whom they despaired of conquering hand to hand.76 Alcibiades, having been awakened by the crackling of the flames, snatched up (as his word had been secretly taken away from him) the side-weapon of a friend of his; for there was with him a certain associate from Arcadia, who would never leave him. This man he desired to follow him, and caught up whatever garments he had at hand, and throwing them out upon the fire, passed through the violence of the flames. When the barbarians saw that he had escaped the conflagration, they killed him by discharging darts at him from a distance,77 and carried his head to Pharnabazus.

A woman, who had been accustomed to live with him, burned his dead body, covered with her own female garments, in the fire of the house which had been prepared to burn him alive. Thus Alcibiades, at the age of about forty, came to his end.

XI. This man, defamed by most writers, three historians of very high authority have extolled with the greatest praises; Thucydides, who was of the same age with him; Theopompus, who was born some time after; and Timaeus; the two latter, though much addicted to censure, have, I know not how, concurred in praising him only; for they have related of him what we have stated above, and this besides, that though he was born in Athens, the most splendid of cities, he surpassed all the Athenians in grandeur and magnificence of living; that when, on being banished from thence, he went to Thebes, he so devoted himself to the pursuits of the Thebans, that no man could match him in laborious exercises and vigour of body, for all the Bœotians cultivate corporeal strength more than mental power; that when he was among the Lacedaemonians, in whose estimation the highest virtue is placed in endurance, he so resigned himself to a hardy way of life, that he surpassed all the Lacedaemonians in the frugality of his diet and living; that when he was among the Thracians, who are hard drinkers and given to lewdness, he surpassed them also in these practices; that when he came among the Persians, with whom it was the chief praise to hunt hard and live high, he so imitated their mode of life, that they themselves greatly admired him in these respects; and that by such conduct, he occasioned that, with whatever people he was, he was regarded as a leading man, and held in the utmost esteem. But we have said enough of him; let us proceed to speak of others.

VIII. THRASYBULUS.

Character of Thrasybulus; he proceeds to deliver his country from the Thirty Tyrants, I.----His success and conduct in the enterprise, II.----His act of oblivion, III.----He is honoured with an olive crown; is killed on the coast of Sicily, IV.

I. THRASYBULUS, the son of Lycus, was a native of Athens. If merit is to be valued by itself, without regard to fortune, I doubt whether I ought not to place him first of all the Greek commanders. This I can say without hesitation, that I set no man above him in integrity, firmness, greatness of mind, and love for his country; for while many have wished, and few have been able, to deliver their country from one tyrant, it was his lot to restore his country, oppressed by thirty tyrants, from slavery to freedom. But though no man excelled him in these virtues, many, I know not how, surpassed him in fame.

First of all, in the Peloponnesian war, he accomplished many undertakings without Alcibiades, while Alcibiades did nothing without him; of all which successes Alcibiades, from certain natural advantages, got the credit. All such actions, however, are common to commanders with their soldiers and with fortune; for, in the shock of battle, the issue is transferred from generalship to the strength and fury of the combatants. The soldier, therefore, of his own right, takes something from the general, and fortune a great deal, and may truly say that she has had more influence on the event than the skill of the commander. This most noble action, then, is entirely Thrasybulus's; for when the Thirty Tyrants, appointed by the Lacedaemonians, kept Athens oppressed in a state of slavery, and had partly banished from their country, and partly put to death, a great number of the citizens whom fortune had spared in the war, and had divided their confiscated property among themselves, he was not only the first, but the only man at the commencement, to declare war against them.

II. When he fled to Phyle, which is a very strong fortress in Attica, he had not more than thirty of his countrymen with him; such was the origin of the deliverance of the Athenians, such the dependence of the liberty of that most famous city. He was at first, indeed, despised by the tyrants, as well as the small number of his followers; which circumstance proved both the ruin of those that despised him, and the security of him that was despised, for it rendered the one party slow to attack, and the other stronger by giving them time for preparation. The maxim, therefore, that "nothing should be despised in war," ought the more deeply to be fixed in the minds of all; and we should remember that it is not said without reason, that "the mother of a cautious person78 is not accustomed to weep." The force of Thrasybulus, however, was not increased in proportion to his expectations; for even in those times good men spoke for liberty with more spirit than they fought for it.

Hence he went to the Piraeeus, and fortified the Munychia,79 which the tyrants twice attempted to storm, but being disgracefully repulsed, and having lost their arms and baggage, they immediately fled back to the city. Thrasybulus, on this occasion, exercised not less prudence than valour; for he forbade those that fled to be injured, thinking it just that "countrymen should spare countrymen;" nor was any one wounded except such as would attack him first. He spoiled no one, as he lay, of his clothes; he laid hands on nothing but arms, of which he was in want, and provisions.80 In the second battle Critias, the leader of the tyrants, was killed, after having, indeed, fought with great bravery against Thrasybulus.

III. Critias being overthrown, Pausanias, king of the Lacedaemonians, came to the support of the Athenians. He made peace between Thrasybulus and those who held the town, on these conditions: "That none should be banished except the Thirty Tyrants, and the Ten, who, having been afterwards made governors, had followed the example of their predecessors in cruelty; 81 that no property should be confiscated; and that the government of the republic should be restored to the hands of the people." It was an honourable act of Thrasybulus, that, when peace was settled, and he had become the most powerful person in the state, he made a law, "that no one should be brought to trial, or punished, for things done previously;" and this they called "the act of oblivion." Nor did he only cause this law to be passed, but also took care that it should be of effect; for when some of them who had been with him in exile, wished to put to death those with whom they had returned to a good understanding, he openly prevented it, and adhered to what he had promised.

IV. For such merits a crown of honour was presented him by the people, made of two sprigs of olive, which, as the love of his countrymen and not force, had procured it him, excited no envy, but was a great glory to him. The celebrated Pittacus, therefore, who was reckoned in the number of the seven wise men, said well, when the Mitylenaeans offered to give him several thousand acres 82 of land, "Do not, I beseech you, give me what many may envy and more may covet; for which reason I had rather take, out of that number, not more than a hundred acres, which will prove both the moderation of my desires and your good will." For small gifts are lasting; but valuable presents are not wont to be permanent. 83 Thrasybulus, accordingly, being content with that crown, neither sought for anything more, nor considered that any one had surpassed him in honour.

Some time after, when, being in command, he had brought up his fleet on the coast of Cilicia, and the watch in his camp was not kept with sufficient care, he was killed in his tent by the barbarians, in a sally made from the town 84 during the night.

IX. CONON.

Conon's services in the Peloponnesian war, I.----In his exile he supports Pharnabazus against the Spartans, II.----He goes to Artaxerxes to accuse Tissaphernes, and treats with him by letter, III.----He defeats the Lacedaemonians at Cnidus; Greece is set free, and the walls of Athens rebuilt, IV.----Conon made prisoner by Tiribazus, V.

I. CONON the Athenian entered upon public life in the Peloponnesian war, and his service in it was of great value; for he was both general of the forces by land, and, as commander of the fleet, performed great exploits by sea; for these reasons particular honour was conferred upon him, for he had the sole authority over all the islands; in which office he took Pherae, a colony of the Lacedaemonians. He was also commander towards the end of the Peloponnesian war, when the forces of the Athenians were defeated by Lysander at Aegospotamos; but he was then absent; and hence the affair was worse managed; for he was both skilled in military matters, and a careful general. It was doubted by nobody, therefore, in those days, that the Athenians, if he had been present, would not have met with that disaster.

II. But when the affairs of the Athenians were in a calamitous condition, and he heard that his native city was besieged, he did not seek a place where he might himself live in security, but one from which he might render assistance to his countrymen. He in consequence betook himself to Pharnabazus, the satrap of Ionia and Lydia, and also a son-in-law and relative of the king, with whom, by much exertion and at great hazard, he contrived to procure himself strong personal influence; 85 for when the Lacedaemonians, after the Athenians were subdued, did not adhere to the alliance which they had made with Artaxerxes, but sent Agesilaus into Asia to make war (being chiefly induced to that course by Tissaphernes, 86 who, from being one of the king's confidants, had renounced his attachment to him, and entered into an alliance with the Lacedaemonians), Pharnabazus was regarded as general against Agesilaus, but Conon in reality led the army, and everything was done according to his direction. He greatly obstructed that eminent commander Agesilaus, and often thwarted his plans. It was indeed apparent, that, if Conon had not been there, Agesilaus would have taken all Asia, as far as Mount Taurus, from the king. And after Agesilaus was recalled home by his countrymen, in consequence of the Boeotians and Athenians having declared war against the Lacedaemonians, Conon nevertheless remained with the king's officers, and was of the greatest service to all of them.

III. Tissaphernes had revolted from the king; yet his defection was not so evident to Artaxerxes as to others; for he had great influence with the king, by reason of his numerous and important services, even when he did not strictly adhere to his duty; nor is it to be wondered at, if he was not easily induced to credit it, remembering that by his means he had overcome his brother Cyrus. Conon, being sent by Pharnabazus to the king to assure him of his guilt, went in the first place, on his arrival (after the manner of the Persians), to Tithraustes, the captain of the guard,87 who held the second place in the empire, and signified that he wished to speak to the king; for no one is admitted without this ceremony.88 Tithraustes answered him, "There is no objection on my part, but consider, for yourself, whether you had rather speak with him, or treat by letter, as to the objects which you have in view For, if you come into the royal presence, it will be necessary for you to pay adoration to the king" (which the Greeks call proskunei=n): "if this is disagreeable to you, you may nevertheless effect what you desire by stating your commission through me." Conon then replied, "To myself indeed, it is not disagreeable to pay any honour you please to the king, but I am afraid lest it should be derogatory to my country, if, coming from a city which has been accustomed to rule over other nations, I should observe the usages of foreigners rather than its own." He therefore delivered to him in writing what he wished to communicate.

IV. The king, having read his statement, was so much influenced by his authority, that he declared Tissaphernes an enemy, desired Conon to harass the Lacedemonians with war, and gave him leave to choose whom be pleased to disburse the money for his army. Conon said that such a choice was not a matter for his consideration, but for the king's own, who ought to know his own subjects best; but that he recommended him to give that commission to Pharnabazus. He was then despatched, after being honoured with valuable presents, to the sea, to require the Cyprians, Phoenicians, and other maritime people, to furnish ships of war, and to prepare a fleet to secure the sea in the following summer, Pharnabazus, as he had requested, being appointed his colleague. When this arrangement was made known to the Lacedaemonians, they took their measures with great care, for they thought that a greater war threatened them than if they had to contend with the Persians only. They saw that a brave and skilful general was going to lead the king's forces, and to take the field against them, a man whom they could overmatch neither by stratagem nor by strength. With these considerations they collected a great fleet, and set sail under the leadership of Pisander. Conon, attacking them near Cnidus, routed them in a great battle, took several of their ships, and sunk several more, a victory by which not only Athens, but also all Greece, which had been under the power of the Lacedaemonians, was set free. Conon proceeded with part of his fleet to his native city, and caused the walls of the Piraeeus and of Athens, both of which had been pulled down, to be rebuilt, and presented to his countrymen fifty talents in money, which he had received from Pharnabazus.

V. What happens to other men happened to him, that he was more inconsiderate in good than in bad fortune; for when he had defeated the fleet of the Peloponnesians, and thought that he had avenged the injuries done to his country, he aimed at more objects than he was in a condition to accomplish. Not that these aims, however, were not patriotic and deserving of praise, since he preferred that the power of his country should be increased, rather than that of the king; for, after he had secured himself great influence by the battle which he fought at Cnidus, not only among foreigners but in all the states of Greece, he began to endeavour secretly 89 to restore Ionia and Aeolia to the Athenians. But as this project was not concealed with sufficient care, Tiribazus, who was governor of Sardis, sent for Conon, on pretence that he wished to send him in great haste to the king; when he had gone, in compliance with this message, he was placed in confinement, in which he was kept for some time. Some have left on record that he was conveyed to the king, and there died. On the other hand Dinon 90 the historian, whom we chiefly credit concerning Persian affairs, has related that he made his escape, but is in doubt whether it was effected with or without the knowledge of Tiribazus.

X. DION.

Dion's family; is connected with the two Dionysii, I.----Brings Plato into Sicily; death of the elder Dionysius, II ---- Disagreement between Dion and Dionysius the Younger, III. ---- Is sent to Corinth; ill-treatment of his wife; fate of his son, IV.----Gets possession of Syracuse, and forces Dionysius to make terms with him, V.----Alienates the people by putting Heraclides to death, VI. ----His great unpopularity, VII.----Is deceived by a stratagem of Callicrates, VIII.----Is assassinated in his own house on a feast-day, IX.----Change of feeling towards him after his death, X.

I. DION, the son of Hipparinus, a native of Syracuse, was of a noble family, and allied to both the Dionysii, the tyrants 91 of Sicily; for the elder married Aristomache, Dion's sister, by whom he had two sons, Hipparinus and Nysaeus, and also two daughters named Sophrosyne and Arete, the elder of whom he gave in marriage to his son Dionysius,92 to whom he also left his dominions, and the other, Arete, to Dion.93

But Dion, besides this noble connexion, and the honourable character of his ancestors, inherited many other advantages from nature; among them, a disposition docile, courteous, and adapted for acquiring the most important branches of knowledge, and extreme grace of person, which is no small recommendation;94 he had also great wealth bequeathed him by his father, which he himself had augmented by the presents he received from the tyrant. He was familiar with the elder Dionysius, not less on account of his character than his relationship; for though the cruelty of Dionysius offended him, yet he was desirous that he should be secure because of his family connexion with himself, and still more for the sake of his own relatives.95 He aided him in important matters, and the tyrant was greatly influenced by his advice, unless, in any case, some violent humour of his own interposed. But embassies,96 such at least as were of a more distinguished kind, were all conducted by Dion; and by discharging them assiduously, and managing faithfully, he palliated the most cruel name of tyrant with his own benevolence. The Carthaginians so much respected him, when he was sent thither by Dionysius, that they never regarded any man that spoke the Greek tongue with more admiration.

II. Nor did these circumstances escape the notice of Dionysius, for he was sensible how great an honour he was to him; hence it happened that he showed him more favour than any other person,97 and loved him not less than a son. When a report reached Sicily, too, that Plato was come to Tarentum, Dionysius could not refuse the young man leave to send for him, as Dion was inflamed with a desire of hearing him. He accordingly granted him that permission, and brought Plato with great pomp 98 to Syracuse; whom Dion so greatly admired and loved, that he devoted himself wholly to his society; nor was Plato less delighted with Dion. Although, therefore, Plato was cruelly insulted by Dionysius (for he ordered him to be sold 99), yet he paid a second visit to the city, induced again by the entreaties of Dion.

In the meantime Dionysius fell ill of some disease, and when he was labouring under the severity of it, Dion inquired of the physicians "how he was," and begged them, at the same time, "if he should happen to be in extreme danger, to acquaint him of it; for he wished to speak to him about a division of the realm, as he thought that the sons of his sister by him ought to have a share in the dominions." This request the physicians did not keep secret, but reported the words to Dionysius the younger, who, taking alarm at it, compelled the physicians to give his father a sleeping potion, that Dion might have no opportunity of addressing him. The sick man, having taken the draught, ended his life like one buried in deep sleep.

III. Such was the commencement of the dissension between Dion and Dionysius; and it was increased by many circumstances, yet in the beginning of his reign there subsisted for a time an assumed friendship between them; and as Dion persisted in soliciting Dionysius to send for Plato from Athens, and follow his counsels, he, who was willing to imitate his father in something, complied with his wishes. At the same time, also, he brought back Philistus the historian to Syracuse, a man not more friendly to the tyrant than to tyranny itself. But of this author more has been said in the work of mine which is written "On Historians." Plato, however, had so much influence over Dionysius by his authority, and produced such an effect on him by his eloquence, that he persuaded him to put an end to his tyranny, and to restore liberty to the Syracusans; but being dissuaded from his intention by the representations of Philistus, he began to grow somewhat more cruel.

IV. Being conscious that he was surpassed by Dion in ability, influence, and in the affection of the people, and fearing that, if he kept Dion with him, he might give him some opportunity of overthrowing him, he gave him a trireme to sail to Corinth, declaring that he did so for both their sakes, lest, as they were afraid of each other, one of them might take the other by surprise. As many people were indignant at this proceeding, and as it was the cause of great hatred to the tyrant, Dionysius put on board some vessels all the property of Dion that could be removed, and sent it after him; for he wished it to be thought that he had adopted that course, not from hatred of the man, but for the sake of his own safety. But when he heard that Dion was levying troops in the Peloponnesus, and endeavouring to raise a war against him, he gave Arete, Dion's wife, in marriage to another man, and caused his son to be brought up in such a manner, that he might, through indulgence, be imbued with the most disgraceful propensities; for mistresses were brought him when but a boy, before he was full grown; he was overwhelmed with wine and luxuries, nor was any time allowed him to be sober. He was so little able to bear such a change in his way of life, which was altered after his father returned to his country (for keepers were set over him to draw him from his former mode of living), that he threw himself from the top of a house and so perished. But I return to the point from whence I digressed.

V. When Dion had arrived at Corinth, and Heraclides, who had been commander of the cavalry, had also come thither (having been likewise banished by Dionysius), they began to prepare for war in every possible way; but they made but little progress; for a tyranny of many years' standing was thought to be of great strength, and for that reason few were induced to join in so perilous an undertaking. But Dion, who trusted not so much to his troops as to the general hatred towards the tyrant, setting out, with the greatest courage, in two transport vessels, to attack a power of fifty years' growth, defended by five hundred ships of war, ten thousand cavalry, and a hundred thousand infantry, so easily made an impression upon it (what seemed wonderful to all people), that he entered Syracuse the third day after he touched the coast of Sicily. Hence it may be understood that no government is safe, unless guarded by the love of its subjects. Dionysius at that time was absent, and waiting for his fleet in Italy, supposing that none of his enemies would come against him without a great force; a supposition which deceived him; for Dion curbed the tyrant's pride with those very men that had been under the rule of his adversary, and gained possession of all that part of Sicily which had been under the government of Dionysius; and with like success he secured the city of Syracuse, except the citadel and the island adjoining the town, and brought matters to such a state, that the tyrant consented to make peace on such terms as these: that Dion should have Sicily, Dionysius Italy,[100] and Apollocrates, in whom alone Dionysius [101] had great confidence, Syracuse.

VI. A sudden change followed close upon such eminent and unexpected success, for fortune, through her fickleness, endeavoured to sink him whom she had just before exalted. In the first place she exercised her power over his son, of whom I have previously made mention; for after he had taken back his wife, who had been given to another, and wished to recall his son, from his abandoned course of sensuality, to habits of virtue, he received, as a father, a most severe affliction in the death of that son. A disagreement next arose between him and Heraclides, who, refusing to yield the supremacy to Dion, organized a party against him; nor had he indeed less influence than Dion among the aristocracy, with whose sanction he commanded the fleet, while Dion had the direction of the land forces. Dion could not endure this opposition patiently, but retorted with that verse of Homer in the second book of the Iliad,[102] in which is this sentiment, "That a state cannot be managed well by the government of many." Much ill feeling, on the part of the people, followed this remark; for he appeared to have let it escape him that he wished everything to be under his own authority. This feeling he did not try to soften by conciliation, but to overcome by severity, and caused Heraclides, when he came to Syracuse, to be put to death.

VII. This act struck extreme terror into every one; for nobody, after Heraclides was killed, considered himself safe. Dion, when his adversary was removed, distributed among his soldiers, with greater freedom, the property of those whom he knew to have been unfavourable to him. But after this division had taken place, money, as his daily expenses grew very great, began to fail him; nor was there anything on which he could lay his hands but the property of his friends; a circumstance which was attended with this effect, that while he gained the soldiery, he lost the aristocracy. At this state of things he was overcome with anxiety, and, being unaccustomed to be ill spoken of, he could not patiently endure that a bad opinion of him should be entertained by those by whose praises he had just before been extolled to the skies. The common people, however, when the feelings of the soldiers were rendered unfavourable towards him,[103] spoke with less restraint, and said that "he was a tyrant not to be endured."

VIII. While he knew not, as he contemplated this state of things, how he should put a stop to it, and was apprehensive as to what it might end in, a certain Callicrates, a citizen of Athens, who had accompanied him from the Peloponnesus to Sicily, a man of address, subtle enough for any artifice, and without any regard for religion or honour, went to him, and told him that "he was in great danger on account of the disaffection of the people and the hostile feelings of the soldiers; which danger he could by no means escape, unless he commissioned some one of his friends to pretend that he was an enemy to him; and that, if he found him fit for the undertaking, he would learn the feelings of every one, and cut off his enemies, as his opponents would readily disclose their thoughts to any one disaffected towards him." This suggestion being approved, Callicrates himself undertook this part, and armed himself through the unsuspiciousness of Dion; he sought for accomplices to join in killing him; he held meetings with his enemies, and formed an actual conspiracy against him. But these proceedings, as many were privy to what was going on, became known, and were communicated to Aristomache, Dion's sister, and his wife Arete; who, being struck with alarm, sought an interview with him for whose danger they were concerned. Dion assured them that no plot was concerted against him by Callicrates, but that what was done, was done by his own directions. The women, notwithstanding, took Callicrates into the temple of Proserpine, and obliged him to swear that "there should be no danger to Dion from him." But Callicrates, by this oath, was not only not deterred from his design, but was stimulated to hasten the execution of it, fearing that his plot might be laid open before he had effected his purpose.

IX. With this resolution, on the next festival day, while Dion was keeping himself at home, secluded from the assembly of the people, and was reposing in an upper room,104 he committed to his accomplices the stronger parts of the city, surrounded Dion's house with guards, and stationed trusty persons at the door, who were not to leave it; he also manned a trireme with an armed force, entrusted it to his brother Philocrates, and gave directions that it should be rowed about in the harbour, as if he wished to exercise the rowers, with a view, if fortune should baffle his attempts, to have a vessel in which he might flee to a place of safety. He then chose from among his followers some young men of Zacynthus, of great courage and extraordinary strength, whom he ordered to go to Dion's house unarmed, so that they might seem to have come for the sake of speaking with him. These youths, as being well known, were admitted, but as soon as they had crossed the threshold, they bolted the door, seized him as he lay on his couch, and bound him. A great noise ensued, so that it was distinctly heard out of doors. And here it was easy to be understood, as has often been said before, how unpopular absolute power is, and how unhappy the life of those who had rather be feared than loved; for those very guards,105 if they had been favourably inclined towards him, might have saved him by breaking open the door, as the Zacynthians, who were unarmed, were holding him still alive, calling to those without for a weapon. Nobody coming to his rescue, one Lyco, a Syracusan, gave them a sword through the window, with which Dion was slain.

X. When the murder was consummated, and the people came in to view the scene, some were killed as guilty by those who were ignorant of the real actors; for a report being soon spread abroad that violence had been offered to Dion, many, to whom such a deed was detestable, ran together to the spot; and these persons, prompted by a false suspicion, killed the innocent as if they had been the delinquents. But as soon as his death became publicly known, the feeling of the populace was wonderfully altered, for those who had called him a tyrant while he was alive, called him now the deliverer of his country and the expeller of a tyrant. So suddenly had pity succeeded to hatred, that they wished to redeem him from Acheron, if they could, with their own blood. He was therefore honoured with a sepulchral monument in the city, in the most frequented part of it, after having been interred at the public expense. He died at the age of about fifty-five years, four years after he had returned from the Peloponnesus into Sicily.

XI. IPHICRATES.

Iphicrates eminent for skill in military discipline, I.----His acts in Thrace, at Corinth, against the Lacedaemonians, in Egypt, and against Epaminondas, II.----His abilities and character, III.

I. IPHICRATES of Athens has become renowned, not so much for the greatness of his exploits, as for his knowledge of military tactics; for he was such a leader, that he was not only comparable to the first commanders of his own time, but no one even of the older generals could be set above him. He was much engaged in the field; he often had the command of armies; he never miscarried in an undertaking by his own fault; he was always eminent for invention, and such was his excellence in it, that he not only introduced much that was new into the military art, but made many improvements in what existed before. He altered the arms of the infantry; for whereas, before he became a commander, they used very large shields, short spears, and small swords, he, on the contrary, introduced the pelta instead of the parma 106 (from which the infantry were afterwards called peltastae), that they might be more active in movements and encounters; he doubled the length of the spear, and made the swords also longer. He likewise changed the character of their cuirasses, and gave them linen ones instead of those of chain-mail and brass; a change by which he rendered the soldiers more active; for, diminishing the weight, he provided what would equally protect the body, and be light.

II. He made war upon the Thracians, and restored Seuthes, the ally of the Athenians, to his throne. At Corinth 107 he commanded the army with so much strictness, that no troops in Greece were ever better disciplined, or more obedient to the orders of their leader; and he brought them to such a habit, that when the signal for battle was given them by their general, they would stand so regularly drawn up, without any trouble on the part of the commander, that they seemed to have been severally posted by the most skilful captain. With this army he cut off a mora 108 of the Lacedaemonians; an exploit which was highly celebrated through all Greece. In this war, too, he defeated all their forces a second time, by which success he obtained great glory.

Artaxerxes, when he had resolved to make war upon the king of Egypt, 109 asked the Athenians to allow Iphicrates to be his general, that he might place him at the head of his army of mercenaries, the number of whom was twelve thousand. This force he so instructed in all military discipline, that as certain Roman soldiers were formerly called Fabians,110 so the Iphicrateans were in the highest repute among the Greeks.

Going afterwards to the relief of the Lacedaemonians, he checked the efforts of Epaminondas; for, had not he been drawing near,111 the Thebans would not have retreated from Sparta until they had taken and destroyed it by fire.

III. He was a man of large mind and large body, and of an appearance indicating the commander so that by his very look he inspired every one with admiration of him. But in action he was too remiss, and too impatient of continued exertion, as Theopompus has recorded. Yet he was a good citizen, and a person of very honourable feelings, as he showed, not only in other transactions, but also in protecting the children of Amyntas 112 the Macedonian; for Eurydice, the mother of Perdiccas and Philip, fled with these two boys, after the death of Amyntas, to Iphicrates, and was secure under his power. He lived to a good old age, with the feelings of his countrymen well affected towards him.

He was once brought to trial for his life, at the time of the Social war, 113 together with Timotheus, and was acquitted.

He left a son named Menestheus, whom he had by a Thracian woman, the daughter of King Cotys. When this son was asked whether he had more regard for his father or his mother, he replied, "For his mother." As this answer appeared strange to all who heard it, he added, "I do so with justice; for my father, as far as was in his power, made me a Thracian, but my mother, as far as she could, made me an Athenian."

XII. CHABRIAS.

Chabrias becomes celebrated for a new mode of fighting, I.----His acts in Egypt and Cyprus; his command of the Egyptian fleet, II.----His recal; he lived but little at home in consequence of the envious feelings of his countrymen, III.----He is killed in the Social war, IV.

I. CHABRIAS the Athenian was also numbered among the most eminent generals, and performed many acts worthy or record. But of these the most famous is his manoeuvre in the battle which he fought near Thebes, when he had gone to the relief of the Boeotians; for in that engagement, when the great general Agesilaus felt sure of victory, and the mercenary troops had been put to flight by him, Chabrias forbade the rest of his phalanx 114 to quit their ground, and instructed them to receive the attack of the enemy with the knee placed firmly against the shield, and the spear stretched out. Agesilaus, observing this new plan, did not dare to advance, and called off his men, as they were rushing forward, with sound of trumpet. This device was so extolled by fame throughout Greece, that Chabrias chose to have the statue, which was erected to him at the public charge by the Athenians in the forum, made in that posture. Hence it happened that wrestlers, and other candidates for public applause,115 adopted, in the erection of their statues, those postures in which they had gained a victory.

II. Chabrias also, when he was general of the Athenians, carried on many wars in Europe; and he engaged in one in Egypt of his own accord; for setting out to assist Nectanabis, 116 he secured him the throne. He performed a similar exploit in Cyprus, but he was then publicly sent to support Evagoras; nor did he return from thence till he had conquered the whole island; from which achievement the Athenians obtained great glory.

In the meantime a war broke out between the Egyptians and Persians, when the Athenians formed an alliance with Artaxerxes, and the Lacedaemonians with the Egyptians, from whom their king Agesilaus received a large share of spoil.117 Chabrias, seeing Agesilaus's good fortune, and thinking himself in no respect inferior to him, set out to assist them of his own accord, and took the command of the Egyptian fleet, while Agesilaus held that of the land forces.

III. In consequence, the officers of the king of Persia sent deputies to Athens, to complain that Chabrias was warring against their king on the side of the Egyptians. The Athenians then prescribed a certain day to Chabrias, before which if he did not return home, they declared that they would condemn him to die. On receiving this communication he returned to Athens; but did not stay there longer than was necessary; for he did not willingly continue under the eyes of his countrymen, as he was accustomed to live splendidly, and to indulge himself too freely to be able to escape the envy of the populace. For this is a common fault in great and free states, that envy is the attendant on glory, and that the people willingly detract from those whom they see raised above others; nor do the poor contemplate with patience the lot of others who are grown rich. Chabrias, therefore, when he could, was generally away from home. Nor was he the only one that willingly absented himself from Athens, but almost all their great men did the same, for they thought that they should be as far removed from envy as they were distant from their native country. Conon, in consequence, lived very much in Cyprus, Iphicrates in Thrace, Timotheus in Lesbos, Chares at Sigeum. Chares, indeed, differed from the others in conduct and character, but was nevertheless both distinguished and powerful at Athens.

IV. Chabrias lost his life in the Social war,118 in the following manner. The Athenians were besieging Chios; Chabrias was on board the fleet as a private man, but had more influence than all who were in command; and the soldiers looked up to him more than to those who were over them. This circumstance hastened his death; for while he was anxious to be the first to enter the harbour, and ordered the captain to steer the vessel towards it, he was the occasion of his own death, since, after he had made his way into it, the other ships did not follow. Upon which, being surrounded by a body of the enemy, his ship, while he was fighting with the utmost bravery, was struck with the beak of one of the enemy's vessels, and began to sink. Though he might have escaped from the danger, if he had cast himself into the sea, for the fleet of the Athenians was at hand to take him up as he swam, he chose rather to die, than to throw away his arms and abandon the vessel in which he had sailed. The others would not act in a similar manner, but gained a place of safety by swimming. He, on the other hand, thinking an honourable death preferable to a dishonourable life, was killed with the weapons of the enemy, while he was fighting hand to hand with them.

XIII. TIMOTHEUS.

The merits and acts of Timotheus, I.----A statue erected to him on his victory over the Lacedaemonians, II.----Is appointed, at an advanced age, as an adviser to Menestheus; is accused by Chares, and condemned, III.----His son Conon obliged to repair the walls of Athens; attachment of Jason to Timotheus, IV.

I. TIMOTHEUS, the son of Conon, a native of Athens, increased the glory which he inherited from his father by many excellent qualities of his own; for he was eloquent, active, persevering, skilled in military affairs, and not less so in managing those of the state. Many honourable actions of his are recorded, the following are the most famous. He subdued the Olynthians and Byzantians by force of arms; he took Samos, on the siege of which, in a previous war, the Athenians had spent twelve hundred talents. This sum he restored 119 to the people without any expense to them; for he carried on a war against Cotys,120 and thence brought twelve hundred talents' worth of spoil into the public treasury. He relieved Cyzicus 121 from a siege; he went with Agesilaus to the assistance of Ariobarzanes; 122 but while the Lacedaemonians received ready money from him in requital, he chose rather to have his countrymen enriched with lands and towns, than to take that of which he himself might carry a share to his own home; and he accordingly received from him Crithote 123 and Sestos.

II. Being made commander of the fleet, and sailing round the Peloponnesus, he laid waste Laconia, and defeated its naval force. He also reduced Corcyra under the power of the Athenians, and attached to them, as allies, the Epirots, the Athamanians, the Chaonians, and all those nations which lie on the sea.124 After this occurrence, the Lacedaemonians desisted from the protracted struggle, and yielded, of their own accord, the sovereignty at sea to the Athenians, making peace upon these terms, "that the Athenians should be commanders by sea." This victory gave so much delight to the Athenians, that altars were then first publicly erected to Peace, and a pulvinar 125 decreed to that goddess. And that the remembrance of this glorious action might be preserved, they raised a statue to Timotheus in the forum at the public expense. Such an honour, that, after the people had erected a statue to the father, they should also present one to the son, happened, down to that period, to him alone. Thus the new statue of the son, placed close by the other, revived old recollections of the father.

III. When he was at an advanced age, and had ceased to hold any office, the Athenians began to be pressed with war on every side. Samos had revolted; the Hellespont 126 had deserted them; Philip of Macedon, then very powerful, was making many efforts; and in Chares,127 who had been opposed to him, there was not thought to be sufficient defence. Menestheus, the son of Iphicrates, and son-in-law of Timotheus, was in consequence made commander, and a decree was passed that he should proceed to take the management of the war. These two persons, his father and father-in-law, men eminent in experience and wisdom, were appointed to give him advice,128 for there was such force of character in them, that great hopes were entertained that what had been lost might be recovered by their means. When they had set out for Samos; and Chares, having heard of their approach, was also proceeding thither with his force, lest anything should appear to be done in his absence, it happened that, as they drew near the island, a great storm arose, which the two veteran commanders, thinking it expedient to avoid, checked the progress of their fleet.129 But Chares, taking a rash course, would not submit to the advice of his elders, but, as if success depended on his own vessel, pushed his way for the point to which he had been steering, and sent orders to Timotheus and Iphicrates to follow him thither. But having subsequently mis-managed the affair, and lost several ships, he returned to the same place 130 from which he had come, and despatched a letter to the government at Athens, saying that it would have been easy for him to take Samos, if he had not been left unsupported by Timotheus and Iphicrates. On this charge they were impeached. The people, violent, suspicious, fickle, and unfavourable to them, recalled them home; and they were brought to trial for treason. On this charge Timotheus was found guilty, and his fine was fixed at a hundred talents; when, compelled by the hatred of an ungrateful people, he sought a refuge at Chalcis.

IV. After his death, when the people had repented of the sentence passed upon him, they took off nine-tenths of the fine, and ordered that his son Conon should give ten talents to repair a certain portion of the wall. In this occurrence was seen the changeableness of fortune; for the grandson was obliged, to the great scandal of his family, to repair, out of his own estate, the same walls which his grandfather Conon had rebuilt with the spoil taken from the enemy.

Of the temperate and judicious life of Timotheus, though we could produce a great many proofs, we will be content with one, from which it may be easily conjectured how dear he was to his friends. When he was brought to trial, while quite a young man, at Athens, not only his friends, and others connected with him by ties of private hospitality, came to give him their support, but among them also the tyrant Jason,131 who at that time was the most powerful of all men. Jason, though he did not think himself safe in his own country without guards, came to Athens unattended, having such value for his guest-friend, that he chose to hazard his life rather than not stand by Timotheus when he was contending for his honour.132 Yet Timotheus, under an order from the people, carried on a war against him afterwards, for he considered the rights of his country more sacred than those of hospitality.

This was the last age of Athenian commanders; the age of Iphicrates, Chabrias, and Timotheus; nor, after their death, was there any leader 133 worthy of remembrance in that city.

XIV. DATAMES.

Datames, an eminent barbarian leader; his war with the Cardusii, I.----He takes prisoner Thyus of Paphlagonia, II.----Presents Thyus to the king of Persia; is appointed to command in Egypt, III.----Is directed to attack Aspis of Cappadocia, IV.----Finds that the courtiers are plotting against him, and takes possession of Cappadocia and Paphlagonia, V.----Loses his son in a war with the Pisidians; defeats the Pisidians, VI.----Is betrayed by his eldest son, VII.----Defeats the general of the Persians who is sent against him, VIII.----Escapes a plot formed against him by the king, IX.----Is deceived by Mithridates, X.----Is killed by him, XI.

I. I NOW come to the bravest and wisest man of all the barbarians, except the two Carthaginians, Hamilcar and Hannibal.

I shall say the more concerning this general, because most of his acts are but little known, and because the undertakings that were attended with success to him, were accomplished, not by vastness of force, but by sagacity, in which he surpassed all of that age; and unless the manner of his proceedings be set forth, his merits cannot be fully understood.

Datames, son of a father named Camissares, a Carian by nation, and of a mother a native of Scythia, served first of all among the soldiers who were guards of the palace to Artaxerxes. His father Camissares, having been found undaunted in fight, active in command, and faithful on many occasions to the king, was granted as a province that portion of Cilicia which borders on Cappadocia, and which the Leucosyrians inhabit.

Datames first showed what sort of man he was, when engaged in military service, in the war which the king carried on against the Cardusii; for in this enterprise, after several thousands of the king's troops were killed, his exertions proved of great value. Hence it happened that, as Camissares lost his life in the war, his father's province was conferred upon him.

II. He distinguished himself by equal valour when Autophradates, by the king's order, made war upon those who had revolted; for the enemy, even after they had entered the camp, were put to flight by his efforts, and the rest of the king's army was saved. In consequence of this success, he began to be appointed over more important affairs. At that time Thyus was prince of Paphlagonia, a man of ancient family, descended from that Pylaemenes whom Homer states to have been killed by Patroclus 134 in the Trojan war. This prince paid no respect to the king's commands. The king, in consequence, determined to make war upon him, and gave the command of the enterprise to Datames, who was a near relative of the Paphlagonian, for they were sons of a brother and a sister. Datames, on this account, was desirous, in the first place, to try every means to bring back his kinsman to his duty without having recourse to arms. But going to confer with him without a guard, as he apprehended no treachery from a friend, he almost lost his life, for Thyus had resolved to assassinate him secretly. Datames was however accompanied by his mother, the aunt of the Paphlagonian, who discovered what was going on, and gave her son warning of it. Datames escaped the danger by flight, and declared open war against Thyus, in which, though he was deserted by Ariobarzanes, the satrap of Lydia, Ionia, and all Phrygia, he nevertheless vigorously persevered, and succeeded in taking Thyus alive with his wife and children.

III. He then used his utmost efforts that the news of his success might not reach the king before him, and thus, while all were still ignorant of it, he arrived at the place where the king was encamped, and the day after arrayed Thyus, a man of huge stature, and frightful aspect, being of a black complexion, and having long hair and a long beard, in a splendid robe such as the king's satraps used to wear. He adorned him also with a chain and bracelets of gold, and other royal ornaments, while he himself was dressed in a coarse thick cloak,135 and rough coat, having a hunter's cap upon his head, a club in his right hand, and in his left a chain, with which he drove Thyus secured before him, as if he were bringing along a wild beast that he had taken. While the people were all gazing at him, on account of the strangeness of his attire, and his person being unknown to them, and a great crowd was in consequence gathered round him, it happened that there was somebody in it who knew Thyus, and went off to tell the king, The king at first did not believe the account, and therefore sent Pharnabazus to make inquiry. Learning from him what had been done, he ordered Datames to be instantly admitted, being extremely delighted both with his success and the dress of his captive, rejoicing especially that that eminent prince had fallen into his hands when he scarcely expected it. He therefore sent Datames, after bestowing magnificent presents upon him, to the army which was then assembling, under the command of Pharnabazus and Tithraus tes, to make war upon Egypt, and directed that he should have equal authority with them. But as the king afterwards recalled Pharnabazus, the chief direction of the war was committed to Datames.

IV. As he was raising an army with the utmost diligence, and preparing to set out for Egypt, a letter was unexpectedly sent him by the king, desiring him to attack Aspis, who then held Cataonia, a country which lies above Cilicia, and borders on Cappadocia. Aspis, occupying a woody country, defended with fortresses, not only refused to obey the king's orders, but ravaged the neighbouring provinces, and intercepted whatever was being conveyed to the king. Datames, though he was far distant from those parts, and was drawn off from a greater matter, yet thought it necessary to yield to the king's wish. He therefore went on board a ship with a few brave followers, thinking (what really happened) that he would more easily overcome him, when unaware of his approach and unprepared, than when ready to meet him, though with ever so great an army. Sailing in this vessel to the coast of Cilicia, landing there, and marching day and night, he passed Mount Taurus, and arrived at the part to which he had directed his course. He inquired where Aspis was, and learned that he was not far off, and was gone to hunt. While he was watching for his return, the cause of his coming became known, and Aspis prepared the Pisidians, and the attendants that he had with him, to offer resistance. When Datames heard this, he took up his arms, and ordered his men to follow him; he himself, setting spurs to his horse, rode on to meet the enemy. Aspis, seeing him, from a distance, advancing upon him, was struck with fear, and, being deterred from his resolution to resist, delivered himself up. Datames consigned him in chains to Mithridates, to be conducted to the king.

V. While these occurrences were passing, Artaxerxes, reflecting from how important a war, and to how inconsiderable an enterprize, he had sent the best of his generals, blamed himself for what he had done, and sent a messenger to the troops at Ace (not supposing that Datames had yet set out), to tell him not to quit the army. But before this messenger arrived at the place to which he was sent, he met upon the road the party that were leading Aspis.

Though Datames, by this celerity, gained great favour from the king, he incurred no less dislike on the part of the courtiers, because they saw that he alone was more valued than all of them; and on this account they all conspired to ruin him. Pandates, the keeper of the king's treasury, a friend to Datames, sent him an account of this state of things in writing, in which he told him that "he would be in great peril if any ill-success should fall out while he commanded in Egypt, for such was the practice of kings, that they attributed adverse occurrences to other men, but prosperous ones to their own good fortune; and hence it happened that they were easily inclined to the ruin of those under whose conduct affairs were said to have been ill-managed; and that he would be in so much the greater danger as he had those for his bitterest enemies to whom the king chiefly gave ear." Datames, having read this letter, after he had arrived at the army at Ace, resolved, as he was aware that what was written was true, to leave the king's service. He did nothing, however, that was unworthy of his honour; for he appointed Mandrocles of Magnesia to command the army, while he himself went off with his adherents into Cappadocia, and took possession of Paphlagonia, that bordered upon it, concealing what his feelings were towards the king. He then privately made a league with Ariobarzanes, raised a force, and assigned the fortified towns to be defended by his own troops.

VI. But these proceedings, from its being winter, went on with but little success. He heard that the Pisidians were raising some forces to oppose him, and sent his son Aridaeus with a detachment against them. The young man fell in battle, and the father marched away to the scene of his death with but a small number of followers, concealing how great a loss he had sustained, for he wished to reach the enemy before the report of his ill-success should become known to his men, lest the spirits of the soldiers should be depressed by hearing of the death of his son. He arrived at the spot to which he had directed his course, and pitched his camp in such a position that he could neither be surrounded by the superior number of the enemy, nor be hindered from keeping his forces always ready to engage. There was with him Mithrobarzanes, his father-in-law, commander of the cavalry, who, despairing of the state of his son-in-law's affairs, went over to the enemy. When Datames heard this, he was sensible that if it should go abroad among the multitude that he was deserted by a man so intimately connected with him, it would happen that others would follow his example. He therefore spread a report throughout the camp that "Mithrobarzanes had gone off as a deserter by his direction, in order that, being received as such, he might the more easily spread destruction among the enemy. It was not right therefore," he added, "that he should be left unsupported, but that they ought all to follow without delay, and, if they did so with spirit, the consequence would be that their foes would be unable to resist, as they would be cut to pieces within their ramparts and without." This exhortation being well received, he led forth his troops, pursued Mithrobarzanes, and, almost at the moment that the latter was joining the enemy,136 gave orders for an attack. The Pisidians, surprised by this new movement, were led to believe that the deserters were acting with bad faith, and by arrangement with Datames, in order that, when received into the camp, they might do them the greater mischief; they therefore attacked them first. The deserters, as they knew not what was in agitation, or why it took place, were compelled to fight with those to whom they had deserted, and to act on the side of those whom they had quitted; and, as neither party spared them, they were quickly cut to pieces. Datames then set upon the rest of the Pisidians who offered resistance, repelled them at the first onset, pursued them as they fled, killed a great number of them, and captured their camp. By this stratagem he at once both cut off the traitors, and overthrew the enemy, and turned to his preservation what had been contrived for his destruction. We have nowhere read, on the part of any commander, any device more ingeniously conceived than this, or more promptly executed.

VII. Yet from such a man as this his eldest son Scismas deserted, and went over to the king, carrying intelligence of his father's defection. Artaxerxes, being startled at this news (for he was aware that he should have to do with a brave and active man, who, when he had conceived a project, had courage to execute it, and was accustomed to think before he attempted to act), despatched Autophradates into Cappadocia. To prevent this general from entering the country, Datames endeavoured to be the first to secure a forest, in which the Gate of Cilicia 137 is situate. But he was unable to collect his troops with sufficient expedition, and being obliged to desist from his attempt, he took up, with the force which he had got together, a position of such a nature, that he could neither be surrounded by the enemy, nor could the enemy pass beyond him without being incommoded by difficulties on both sides; while, if he wished to engage with them, the numbers of his opponents could not greatly damage his own smaller force.

VIII. Autophradates, though he was aware of these circumstances, yet thought it better to fight than to retreat with so large an army, or to continue inactive so long in one place. He had twenty thousand barbarian cavalry, a hundred thousand infantry, whom they call Cardaces,138 and three thousand slingers of the same class. He had besides eight thousand Cappadocians, ten thousand Armenians, five thousand Paphlagonians, ten thousand Phrygians, five thousand Lydians, about three thousand Aspendians and Pisidians, two thousand Cilicians, as many Captianians,139 three thousand hired men from Greece, and a very large number of light-armed troops. Against this force all Datames's hopes rested on himself and the nature of his ground, for he had not the twentieth part of his enemy's numbers. Trusting to himself and his position,140 therefore, he brought on a battle, and cut off many thousands of the enemy, while there fell of his own army not more than a thousand men; on which account he erected a trophy the next day on the spot where they had fought the day before. When he had moved his camp from thence, and always, though inferior in forces, came off victorious in every battle (for he never engaged but when he had confined his adversaries in some defile, an advantage which often happened to one acquainted with the ground and taking his measures with skill), Autophradates, seeing that the war was protracted with more loss to the king than to the enemy, exhorted Datames to peace and friendship,141 so that he might again be received into favour with the king. Datames, though he saw that peace would not be faithfully kept, nevertheless accepted the offer of it, and said that "he would send deputies to Artaxerxes." Thus the war, which the king had undertaken against Datames, was ended; and Autophradates retired into Phrygia.

IX. But the king, as he had conceived an implacable hatred to Datames, endeavoured, when he found that he could not be overcome in the field, to cut him off by underhand artifices; but most of these he eluded. For instance, when it was told him that some, who were reckoned in the number of his friends, were laying a plot for him (concerning whom, as their enemies were the informers, he thought that the intimation was neither entirely to be believed nor utterly disregarded), he resolved to make trial whether what had been told him was true or false. He accordingly went forward on the road on which they had stated that an ambush would be laid for him; but he selected a man closely resembling himself in person and stature, gave him his own attire, and ordered him to ride on in that part of the line where he himself had been accustomed to go, while Datames himself, in the equipments and dress of a common soldier, prepared to march among his own body-guard. The men in ambuscade, as soon as the party reached the spot where they were stationed, being deceived by the place and dress, made an assault upon him who had been substituted for Datames. But Datames had previously directed those among whom he was marching, to be ready to do what they should see him do. He, as soon as he saw the conspirators collecting in a body, hurled his darts among them, and, as all the rest did the same, they fell down dead before they could reach him whom they meant to attack.

X. Yet this man, crafty as he was, was at last ensnared by a device of Mithridates, the son of Ariobarzanes; for Mithridates promised the king that he would kill Datames, if the king would allow him to do with impunity whatever he wished, and would give him a pledge to that effect with his right hand after the manner of the Persians. When he received this pledge sent him by the king,142 he prepared a force, and though at a distance, made a league with Datames, ravaged the king's provinces, stormed his fortresses, and carried off a great quantity of spoil, part of which he divided among his men, and part he sent to Datames, putting into his hands, in like manner, many strong-holds. By pursuing this course for a long time, he made Datames believe that he had undertaken an everlasting war against the king, while notwithstanding (lest he should raise in him any suspicion of treachery), he neither sought a conference with him, nor showed any desire to come into his sight. Thus, though keeping at a distance, he maintained friendship with him; but so that they seemed to be bound to one another, not by mutual kindnesses, but by the common hatred which they had conceived towards the king.

XI. When he thought that he had sufficiently established this notion, he gave intimation to Datames that it was time for greater armies to be raised, and an attack to be made on the king himself; and that, with reference to this subject, he might, if he pleased, come to a conference with him in any place that he might choose. The proposal being accepted, a time was fixed for the conference, and a place in which they were to meet. To this spot Mithridates came some days previously, in company with a person in whom he had the greatest confidence, and buried swords in several different places, carefully marking each spot. On the day of the conference, each of them brought people to examine the place, and to search Datames and Mithridates themselves. They then met, and after they had spent some time in conference, and parted in different directions, and Datames was some distance off, Mithridates, before he went back to his attendants (lest he should excite any suspicion), returned to the same place, and sat down, as if he wished to rest from weariness, on one of the spots in which a sword had been concealed, and, at the same time, called back Datames, pretending that he had forgotten something at their conference. In the mean time he drew out the sword that was hid, and concealed it, unsheathed, under his garment, and observed to Datames, as he was returning, that he had noticed, when going off, that a certain place, which was in sight, was suitable for pitching a camp. While he was pointing this out with his finger, and the other was looking towards it, he ran him through, as his back was turned, with the sword, and put an end to his life before any one could come to his assistance. Thus a man who had gained the mastery over many by prudence, over none by treachery, was ensnared by pretended friendship.

XV. EPAMINONDAS

Remarks on the manners of the Greeks, I.----Youth and manhood of Epaminondas, II.----Excellencies of his character, III.----An instance of his freedom from covetousness, IV.----His ability in speaking, V.----An instance of his power of persuasion; the battle of Leuctra, VI.----His patriotism; his care for the army and its success, VII.----Is brought to trial for retaining his command longer than the law allowed; his defence and acquittal, VIII.----His death at Mantinea, IX.----His apology for not marrying; his horror of civil bloodshed; the glory of Thebes, X.

I. EPAMINONDAS was the son of Polymnis, and was born at Thebes. Before we proceed to write of him, the following caution seems necessary to be given to our readers; that they should not confound the customs of other nations with their own, or think that those things which appear unimportant to themselves must be equally so to others. We know that skill in music, according to our habits, is foreign to the character of any eminent personage; and that to dance is accounted disparaging to the character; 143 while all such accomplishments among the Greeks are regarded both as pleasing and as worthy of admiration.

But as we wish to draw a correct picture of the habits and life of Epaminondas, we seem called upon to omit nothing that may tend to illustrate it. We shall therefore speak in the first place of his birth; we shall then show in what accomplishments, and by whom, he was instructed; next we shall touch upon his manners and intellectual endowments, and whatever other points in his character may deserve notice; and lastly on his great actions, which are more regarded by many than all the best qualities of the mind.144

II. He was the son, then, of the father whom we named, and was of an honourable family, though left poor by his ancestors; but he was so well educated that no Theban was more so; for he was taught to play upon the harp, and to sing to the sound of its strings, by Dionysius, who was held in no less honour among musicians than Damon or Lamprus,145 whose names are well known; to play on the flutes 146 by Olympiodorus; and to dance by Calliphron. For his instructor in philosophy he had Lysis 147 of Tarentum, a Pythagorean, to whom he was so devoted that, young as he was, he preferred the society of a grave and austere old man 148 before that of all those of his own age; nor did he part with him until he so far excelled his fellow students in learning, that it might easily be perceived he would in like manner excel them all in other pursuits. These acquirements, according to our habits, are trifling, and rather to be despised; 149 but in Greece, at least in former times, they were a great subject for praise. After he grew up, and began to apply himself to gymnastic exercises, he studied not so much to increase the strength, as the agility, of his body; for he thought that strength suited the purposes of wrestlers, but that agility conduced to excellence in war. He used to exercise himself very much, therefore, in running and wrestling, as long as 150 he could grapple, and contend standing, with his adversary. But he spent most of his labour on martial exercises.

III. To the strength of body thus acquired were added many good qualities of the mind; for he was modest, prudent, grave, wisely availing himself of opportunities, skilled in war, brave in action, and possessed of remarkable courage; he was so great a lover of truth, that he would not tell a falsehood even in jest; he was also master of his passions, gentle in disposition, and patient to a wonderful degree, submitting to wrong, not only from the people, but from his own friends; he was a remarkable keeper of secrets, a quality which is sometimes not less serviceable than to speak eloquently; and he was an attentive listener to others, because he thought that by this means knowledge was most easily acquired. Whenever he came into a company, therefore, in which a discussion was going on concerning government, or a conversation was being held on any point of philosophy, he never went away till the discourse was brought to its conclusion. He bore poverty so easily, that he received nothing from the state but glory. He did not avail himself of the means of his friends to maintain himself; but he often used his credit to relieve others, to such a degree that it might be thought all things were in common between him and his friends; for when any one of his countrymen had been taken by the enemy, or when the marriageable daughter of a friend could not be married for want of fortune, he used to call a council of his friends, and to prescribe how much each should give according to his means; and when he had made up the sum required, he brought the man who wanted it to those who contributed, and made them pay it to the person himself, in order that he, into whose hands the sum passed, might know to whom he was indebted, and how much to each.

IV. His indifference to money was put to the proof by Diomedon of Cyzicus; for he, at the request of Artaxerxes, had undertaken to bribe Epaminondas. He accordingly came to Thebes with a large sum in gold, and, by a present of five talents, brought over Micythus, a young man for whom Epaminondas had then a great affection, to further his views. Micythus went to Epaminondas, and told him the cause of Diomedon's coming. But Epaminondas, in the presence of Diomedon, said to him, "There is no need of money in the matter; for if what the king desires is for the good of the Thebans, I am ready to do it for nothing; but if otherwise, he has not gold and silver enough to move me, for I would not accept the riches of the whole world in exchange for my love for my country. At you, who have made trial of me without knowing my character, and have thought me like yourself, I do not wonder; and I forgive you: but quit the city at once, lest you should corrupt others though you have been unable to corrupt me. You, Mycithus, give Diomedon his money back; or, unless you do so immediately, I shall give you up to the magistrates." Diomedon entreating that he might be allowed to depart in safety, and carry away with him what he had brought, "That," he replied, "I will grant you, and not for your sake, but for my own, lest any one, if your money should be taken from you, should say that what I would not receive when offered me, had come into my possession after being taken out of yours." Epaminondas then asking Diomedon "whither he wished to be conducted," and Diomedon having answered, "To Athens," he gave him a guard in order that he might reach that city in safety. Nor did he, indeed, think that precaution sufficient, but also arranged, with the aid of Chabrias the Athenian, of whom we have spoken above, that he should embark without molestation. Of his freedom from covetousness this will be a sufficient proof. We might indeed produce a great number; but brevity must be studied, as we have resolved to comprise, in this single volume, the lives of several eminent men, whose biographies many writers before us have related at great length.151

V. He was also an able speaker, so that no Theban was a match for him in eloquence; nor was his language less pointed in brief replies than elegant in a continued speech. He had for a traducer, and opponent in managing the government, a certain Meneclidas, also a native of Thebes,152 a man well skilled in speaking, at least for a Theban, for in that people is found more vigour of body than of mind. He, seeing that Epaminondas was distinguished in military affairs, used to advise the Thebans to prefer peace to war, in order that his services as a general might not be required. Epaminondas in consequence said to him, "You deceive your countrymen with words, in dissuading them from war, since under the name of peace you are bringing upon them slavery; for peace is procured by war, and they, accordingly, who would enjoy it long, ought to be trained to war. If therefore, my countrymen, you wish to be leaders of Greece, you must devote yourselves to the camp, not to the palaestra."153 When this Meneclidas also upbraided him with having no children, and with not having taken a wife, and, above all, with presumption in thinking that he had acquired the glory of Agamemnon in war, "Forbear," he rejoined, "Meneclidas, to reproach me with regard to a wife, for I would take nobody's advice on that subject less willingly than yours;" (for Meneclidas lay under a suspicion of making too free with other men's wives;) "and as to supposing that I am emulous of Agamemnon, you are mistaken; for he, with the support of all Greece, hardly took one city in ten years; I, on the contrary with the force of this one city of ours, and in one day, delivered all Greece by defeating the Lacedaemonians."

VI. When Epaminondas went to the public assembly of the Arcadians, to request them to join in alliance with the Thebans and Argives, and Callistratus, the ambassador from the Athenians, who excelled all men of that day in eloquence, begged of them, on the other hand, rather to unite in alliance with Athens, and uttered many invectives against the Thebans and Argives, and among them made this remark, "that the Arcadians ought to observe what sort of citizens each city had produced, from whom they might form a judgment of the rest; for that Orestes and Alcmaeon, murderers of their mothers, were Argives, and that Oedipus, who, when he had killed his father, had children by his mother, was born at Thebes." Upon this,154 Epaminondas, in his reply, when he had done speaking as to other points, and had come to those two grounds of reproach, said that "he wondered at the simplicity of the Athenian rhetorician, who did not consider that those persons, to whom he had alluded, were born innocent, and that, after having been guilty of crimes at home, and having in consequence been banished from their country, they had been received by the Athenians." 155

But his eloquence shone most at Sparta (when he was ambassador before the battle of Leuctra), 156 where, when the ambassadors from all the allies had met, Epaminondas, in a full assembly of the embassies, so clearly exposed the tyranny of the Lacedaemonians, that he shook their power by that speech not less than by the battle of Leuctra; for he was at that time the cause (as it afterwards appeared) that they were deprived of the support of their allies.

VII. That he was of a patient disposition, and ready to endure wrongs from his countrymen, because he thought it species of impiety to show resentment towards his country, there are the following proofs. When the Thebans, from some feeling of displeasure towards him, refused to place him at the head of the army,157 and a leader was chosen that was ignorant of war, by whose mismanagement that great multitude of soldiers was brought to such a condition that all were alarmed for their safety, as they were confined within a narrow space and blocked up by the enemy, the energy of Epaminondas began to be in request (for he was there as a private 158 among the soldiers), and when they desired aid from him, he showed no recollection of the affront that had been put upon him, but brought the army, after releasing it from the blockade, safely home. Nor did he act in this manner once only, but often; 159 but the most remarkable instance was, when he had led an army into the Peloponnesus against the Lacedaemonians, and had two joined in command with him, of whom one was Pelopidas, a man of valour and activity;----on this occasion, when, through the accusations of their enemies, they had all fallen under the displeasure of their countrymen, and their commission was in consequence taken from them, and other commanders came to take their place, Epaminondas did not obey the order of the people, and persuaded his colleagues to follow his example, continuing to prosecute the war which he had undertaken, for he saw that, unless he did so, the whole army would be lost through the incautiousness and ignorance of its leaders. But there was a law at Thebes, which punished any one with death who retained his command longer than was legally appointed. Epaminondas, however, as he saw that this law had been made for the purpose of preserving the state, was unwilling to make it contribute to its ruin, and continued to exercise his command four months longer than the people had prescribed.

VIII. When they returned home, his colleagues 160 were impeached for this offence, and he gave them leave to lay all the blame upon him, and to maintain that it was through his means that they did not obey the law. They being freed from danger by this defence, nobody thought that Epaminondas would make any reply, because, as was supposed, he would have nothing to say. But he stood forward on the trial, denied nothing of what his adversaries laid to his charge, and admitted the truth of all that his colleagues had stated; nor did he refuse to submit to the penalty of the law; but he requested of his countrymen one favour, namely, that they would inscribe in their judicial record of the sentence passed upon him, 161 "Epaminondas was punished by the Thebans with death, because he obliged them to overthrow the Lacedaemonians at Leuctra, whom, before he was general, none of the Boeotians durst look upon in the field, and because he not only, by one battle, rescued Thebes from destruction, but also secured liberty for all Greece, and brought the power of both people to such a condition, that the Thebans attacked Sparta, and the Lacedaemonians were content if they could save their lives; nor did he cease to prosecute the war, till, after settling Messene,162 he shut up Sparta with a close siege." When he had said this, there burst forth a laugh from all present, with much merriment, and no one of the judges ventured to pass sentence upon him. Thus he came off from this trial for life with the greatest glory.

IX. When, towards the close of his career, he was commander at Mantinea, and, pressing very boldly upon the enemy with his army in full array, was recognized by the Lacedaemonians, they directed their efforts in a body against him alone, because they thought the salvation of their country depended upon his destruction, nor did they fall back, until, after shedding much blood, and killing many of the enemy, they saw Epaminondas himself, while fighting most valiantly, fall wounded with a spear hurled from a distance. By his fall the Boeotians were somewhat disheartened; yet they did not quit the field till they had put to flight those opposed to them. As for Epaminondas himself, when he found that he had received a mortal wound, and also that if he drew out the iron head of the dart, which had stuck in his body, he would instantly die, he kept it in until it was told him that "the Boeotians were victorious." When he heard these words, he said "I have lived long enough; for I die unconquered." The iron head being then extracted, he immediately died.

X. He was never married; and when he was blamed on this account (as he would leave no children 163) by Pelopidas, who had a son of bad character, and who said that he, in this respect, but ill consulted the interest of his country, "Beware," he replied, "lest you should consult it worse, in being about to leave behind you a son of such a reputation. But neither can

I," he added, "want issue; for I leave behind me a daughter, the battle of Leuctra, that must of necessity not only survive me, but must be immortal."

At the time when the Theban exiles, under the leadership of Pelopidas, possessed themselves of Thebes, and expelled the garrison of the Lacedaemonians from the citadel, Epaminondas, as long as the slaughter of the citizens continued, confined himself to his own house, for he would neither defend the unworthy, nor attack them, that he might not stain his hands with the blood of his own countrymen. But when the struggle began at the Cadmea 164 with the Lacedaemonians, he took his stand among the foremost.

Of his merits and his life enough will have been said, if I add but this one remark, of which none can deny the truth; that Thebes, as well before Epaminondas was born, as after his death, was always subject to some foreign power, 165 but that, as long as he held the reigns of government, it was the head of all Greece. Hence it may be understood, that one man was of more efficacy than the whole people.

XVI. PELOPIDAS.

Phoebidas seizes on the citadel of Thebes; Pelopidas banished, I.----Pelopidas, with twelve followers, effects a return to Thebes, II.----He delivers his country from the Lacedaemonians, expelling their garrison, III.----His acts in conjunction with Epaminondas, IV.----His contest with Alexander of Pherae; his death, V.

I. PELOPIDAS, of Thebes, is better known to those acquainted with history than to the multitude. As to his merits, I am in doubt how I shall speak of them; for I fear that, if I begin to give a full account of his actions, I may seem, not to be relating his life, but to be writing a history, or that, if I touch only on his principal exploits, it may not clearly appear to those ignorant of Grecian literature how great a man he was, I will therefore, as far as I can, meet both difficulties, and provide against the satiety, as well as for the imperfect knowledge, of my readers.

Phoebidas, the Lacedaemonian, when he was leading an army to Olynthus,166 and marching through the territory of Thebes,167 possessed himself (at the instigation of a few of the Thebans, who, the better to withstand the opposite faction, favoured the interest of the Lacedaemonians,) of the citadel of Thebes, which is called the Cadmea,168 and this he did of his own private determination, not from any public resolution of his countrymen. For this act the Lacedaemonians removed him from his command of the army, and fined him a sum of money, but did not show the more inclination, on that account, to restore the citadel to the Thebans, because, as enmity had arisen between them, they thought it better that they should be under a check than left at liberty; for, after the Peloponnesian war was ended, and Athens subdued, they supposed that the contest must be between them and the Thebans, and that they were the only people who would venture to make head against them. With this belief they committed the chief posts to their own friends, while they partly put to death, and partly banished, the leading men of the opposite party; and amongst them Pelopidas, of whom we have begun to write, was expelled from his country.

II. Almost all these exiles had betaken themselves to Athens, not that they might live in idleness, but that, whatever opportunity chance should first offer, they might avail themselves of it to regain their country.169 As soon, therefore, as it seemed time for action, they, in concert with those who held similar views at Thebes, fixed on a day for cutting off their enemies and delivering their country, and made choice of that very day on which the chief magistrates were accustomed to meet at a banquet together. Great exploits have been often achieved with no very numerous forces, but assuredly never before was so great a power overthrown from so small a beginning. For, out of those who had been banished, twelve young men (there not being in all more than a hundred who were willing to encounter so great a danger,) agreed to attempt the enterprise; and by this small number the power of the Lacedaemonians was overcome; for these youths made war on that occasion, not more upon the faction of their adversaries than upon the Spartans, who were lords of Greece, and whose imperious domination, shaken by this commencement, was humbled not long after in the battle of Leuctra.

These twelve, then, whose leader was Pelopidas, quitting Athens in the day-time, with a view to reach Thebes when the sky was obscured by evening, set out with hunting dogs, carrying nets in their hands, and in the dress of countrymen, in order that they might accomplish their journey with less suspicion. Having arrived at the very time that they had desired, they proceeded to the house of Charon, by whom the hour and day 170 had been fixed.

III. Here I would observe in passing, although the remark be unconnected with the subject before us,171 how great mischief excessive confidence is wont to produce; for it soon came to the ears of the Theban magistrates that some of the exiles had entered the city, but this intelligence, being intent upon their wine and luxuries, they so utterly disregarded, that they did not take the trouble even to inquire about so important a matter. Another circumstance was added, too, which may show their folly in a more remarkable light. A letter was brought from Athens by Archias the hierophant,172 to Archias, who then held the chief post at Thebes, in which a full account had been written concerning the expedition of the exiles. This letter being delivered to Archias as he was reclining at the banquet, he, thrusting it under the bolster, sealed as it was, said, "I put off serious matters till to-morrow." But those revellers, when the night was far advanced, and they were overcome with wine, were all put to death by the exiles under the command of Pelopidas. Their object being thus effected, and the common people being summoned to take arms and secure their liberty, not only those who were in the city, but also others from all parts out of the country, flocked together to join them; they then expelled the garrison of the Lacedaemonians from the citadel, and delivered their country from thraldom. The promoters of the seizure of the Cadmea they partly put to death, and partly sent into exile.

IV. During this period of turbulence, Epaminondas, as we have already observed, remained quiet, so long as the struggle was between fellow-citizens, in his own house. The glory of delivering Thebes, therefore, belongs wholly to Pelopidas; almost all his other honours were gained in conjunction with, Epaminondas. In the battle of Leuctra, where Epaminondas was commander-in-chief, Pelopidas was leader of a select body of troops, which were the first to bear down the phalanx of the Spartans. He was present with him, too, in all his dangers. When he attacked Sparta, he commanded one wing of the army; and, in order that Messene might be sooner restored,173 he went ambassador to Persia. He was, indeed, the second of the two great personages at Thebes, but second only in such a way that he approached very near to Epaminondas.

V. Yet he had to struggle with adverse fortune. He lived in exile, as we have shown, in the early part of his life; and, when he sought to bring Thessaly under the power of the Thebans, and thought that he was sufficiently protected by the law of embassies, which used to be held sacred by all nations, he was seized, together with Ismenias, by Alexander, tyrant of Pherae, and thrown into prison. Epaminondas, making war upon Alexander, restored him to liberty. But after this occurrence, he could never be reconciled in feeling to him by whom he had been unjustly treated. He therefore persuaded the Thebans to go to the relief of Thessaly, and to expel its tyrants. The chief command in the expedition being given to him, and he having gone thither with an army, he did not hesitate to come to a battle the moment he saw the enemy. In the encounter, as soon as he perceived Alexander, he spurred on his horse, in a fever of rage, to attack him, and, separating too far from his men, was killed by a shower of darts. This happened when victory was in his favour, for the troops of the tyrant had already given way. Such being the event, all the cities of Thessaly honoured Pelopidas, after his death, with golden crowns and brazen statues, and presented his children with a large portion of land.

XVII. AGESILAUS.

Agesilaus elected king of Sparta, his brother's son being set aside, I.----His expedition to Asia; his strict observance of his truce with Tissaphernes, II.----He lays waste Phrygia; winters at Ephesus; deceives Tissaphernes, III.----Is recalled to defend his country; defeats the Thebans at Coronea; his clemency, IV.----His success in the Corinthian war; spares Corinth, V.----Refuses to go to the battle at Leuctra; saves Sparta by a stratagem, VI.----Replenishes the treasury of his country, VII.----His personal appearance and mode of life; his death at the harbour of Menelaus, VIII.

AGESILAUS the Lacedaemonian has been praised not only by other writers, but, above all, by Xenophon, the disciple of Socrates, for he treated Xenophon as an intimate friend.

In his early days he had a dispute with Leotychides, his brother's son, about the throne; for it was a custom handed down among the Lacedaemonians from their ancestors, that they should always have two kings, in name rather than power, of the two families of Procles and

Eurysthenes, who were the first kings of Sparta, of the progeny of Hercules. It was not lawful for a king to be made out of one of these families instead of the other; each of the two, therefore, maintained its order of succession. Regard was had, in the first place, to the eldest of the sons of him who died while on the throne; but if he had left no male issue, the choice then fell on him who was next of kin. King Agis, the brother of Agesilaus, had recently died, and had left a son named Leotychides, whom, during his life, he had not acknowledged, but, at his death, had declared to be his. Leotychides contended for the royal dignity with his uncle Agesilaus, but did not obtain what he sought, for Agesilaus was preferred through the interest of Lysander, a man, as we have already stated, of a factious character, and at that time of great influence.

II. Agesilaus, as soon as he got possession of the throne, solicited the Lacedaemonians to send an army into Asia, and make war upon the king of Persia, assuring them that it was better to fight in Asia than in Europe; for a rumour had gone abroad that Artaxerxes was equipping a fleet, and raising land forces, to send into Greece. Permission being granted him, he exerted so much expedition, that he arrived in Asia with his troops before the king's satraps knew that he had set out; hence it happened that he surprised them all unprepared, and expecting nothing of the kind. But as soon as Tissaphernes, who had the chief authority among the royal satraps, heard of his arrival, he begged a truce of the Spartan, on pretence that he would try to effect an agreement between the Lacedaemonians and the king, but in reality to gain time for collecting troops; and he obtained a truce for three months. Each of them, however, took an oath to observe the truce without fraud; to which engagement Agesilaus adhered with the greatest honour; but Tissaphernes, on the other hand, did nothing but make preparations for war. Though Agesilaus became aware of his proceedings, he still kept his oath, and said that "he was a great gainer by doing so, for Tissaphernes, by his perjury, both alienated men from his interest, and made the gods angry with him; while he, by being faithful to his obligation, produced confidence among his troops, as they felt that the power of the gods was on their side, and that men were rendered greater friends to them, because they were accustomed to favour those whom they saw keeping faith."

III. When the period of the truce was expired, the barbarian, not doubting that as he had many residences in Caria, and as that province was then thought by far the richest in Asia, the enemy would direct their attacks on that quarter especially, assembled his whole force on that side. But Agesilaus turned into Phrygia, and laid waste the country before Tissaphernes could make a movement in any direction. After enriching his men with abundance of plunder, he led back his army to Ephesus to winter, and erecting forges for arms there, made preparations for war with great industry. That his soldiers might be armed with greater care, too, and equipped with more display, he proposed rewards, with which those were to be presented whose efforts to that end should be remarkably distinguished. He pursued the same course with regard to different kinds of exercises, so as to honour with valuable gifts those who excelled others in them. By this means he succeeded in getting an army most admirably accoutred and trained.

When he thought it time to draw his troops out of winter quarters, he saw that if he openly declared in what direction he was going to march, the enemy would not give credit to his statement, but would occupy other parts with their forces, not doubting that he would do something quite different from what he said. Agesilaus, accordingly, giving out that he would march for Sardis, Tissaphernes felt convinced that Caria must again be defended. When his expectation deceived him in the matter, and he found himself outwitted by his adversary's shrewdness, he hastened to protect his dependants, but too late, for, when he arrived, Agesilaus had taken many places, and secured abundance of spoil.

The Lacedaemonian king, seeing that the enemy were superior to him in cavalry, never gave them an opportunity of attacking him in the plains, but engaged them in those parts in which infantry would be of greater service. As often as he came to a battle, therefore, he routed forces of the enemy far more numerous than his own; and he so conducted himself in Asia that he was in the judgment of every one accounted superior to his opponent.

IV. While he was thinking of marching into Persia, and attacking the king himself, a messenger came to him from home, by order of the Ephori, to acquaint him that the Athenians and Boeotians had declared war against the Lacedaemonians, and that he should therefore not delay to return. In this juncture is dutifulness to his country is not less to be admired than his merit in war, for though he was at the head of a victorious army, and felt assured, to the utmost, of becoming master of the kingdom of Persia, he obeyed the orders of the absent magistrates with as much respect as if he had been a private person in the comitium 174 at Sparta. Would that our generals had followed his example! But let us proceed with our subject. Agesilaus preferred an honourable name to the most powerful empire, and thought it much more glorious to obey the laws of his country than to subdue Asia in war. With these feelings, therefore, he led his forces over the Hellespont, and employed such expedition, that he accomplished in thirty days a journey which Xerxes had taken a year to perform.175 When he was not very far from the Peloponnesus, the Athenians and Boeotians, and others in alliance with them, endeavoured to make a stand against him at Coronea, all of whom he defeated in a great battle. It was an eminent merit in his victory, that when a numerous body of the enemy had taken refuge in a temple of Minerva after the defeat, and the question was put to him, "what he would wish to be done with them," he, though he had received some wounds in the battle, and seemed angry with all who had borne arms against him, preferred, nevertheless, respect for religion to the gratification of his resentment, and gave orders that they should suffer no injury. Nor did he act thus in Greece only,----so as to save the temples of the gods from profanation,----but even among the barbarians also, he preserved every image and altar with the utmost scrupulosity. He used publicly to observe, therefore, that "he wondered those were not counted in the number of the sacrilegious who injured the suppliants of the gods,176 or that those who lessened respect for religion were not visited with severer punishments than those who robbed temples."

V. After this battle all the war was concentrated about Corinth, and was accordingly called the Corinthian war. During this contest, when, in one battle, in which Agesilaus was general,177 there had fallen ten thousand of the enemy, and the strength of his opponents seemed broken by that catastrophe, he was so far from presumptuous boasting,178 that he expressed commiseration for the fortune of Greece, since it was through the fault of his enemies that so many had been defeated and killed by him, for with that number, if the mind of his adversaries had been but right, the Persians might have been forced to make atonement to Greece. When he had driven the enemy, too, within their walls, and many exhorted him to attack Corinth, he said, "that it would not be consistent with his character in war to do so; since he was one," he said, "who would oblige offenders to return to their duty, not one who would destroy the noblest cities of Greece; for if we should proceed," he added, "to extirpate those who have supported us against the barbarians, we should weaken ourselves while the barbarians remain at their ease; and, when this has taken place, they will easily bring us under their power whenever they please."

VI. In the mean time the disaster at Leuctra befel the the Lacedaemonians; and that he might not march thither,179 though he was urged by many to go to the field, he refused to go, as if he had a presentiment concerning the event. But when Epaminondas attacked Sparta, and the city was without walls, he proved himself such a commander, that it was apparent to all on that occasion, that if it had not been for him, Sparta would have ceased to exist.180 In this time or danger, indeed, the celerity of his proceedings was the preservation of the whole people; for when a number of the young men, alarmed at the approach of the enemy, had determined on going over to the Thebans, and had taken a position on an eminence without the city, Agesilaus, who saw that it would have a most pernicious effect, if it were noticed that any were trying to desert to the enemy, went thither with some of his men, and, as if they had been acting with a good intention, commended their procedure in having taken possession of that spot, and said that he himself had also observed that this ought to be done. Thus, by his pretended commendation, he prevented the young men from deserting, and, after joining some of his followers with them, left the place quite safe, for when the number of those was increased who were unacquainted with the project,181 the conspirators were afraid to move, and retained their ground the more willingly as they thought that what they had meditated was still unknown.

VII. After the battle of Leuctra, it is certain, the Lacedaemonians never recovered themselves, or regained their former power, though, at that period, Agesilaus did not cease to assist his country by whatever means he could use. When the Lacedaemonians were greatly in want of money, he gave his support to all those 182 who had revolted from the king, and being presented by them with a large sum, he relieved his country with it. In his character, indeed, this point was particularly worthy of admiration, that, though great presents were given him by kings, princes, and states, he never took any portion of them into his own house, and never departed in the least from the usual diet and dress of the Spartans; he remained content with the same house which Eurysthenes, the progenitor of his family, had inhabited; and whoever entered it could see no indication of luxury or extravagance, but, on the contrary, many proofs of temperance and frugality, for it was furnished in such a manner that it differed in no respect from that of any poor or private person.

VIII. As this great man had found nature favourable in giving him excellent qualities of mind, so he found her unpropitious with regard to the formation of his body; for he was of low stature, small in person, and lame of one foot. These circumstances rendered his appearance the reverse of attractive, and strangers, when they looked at his person, felt only contempt for him, while those who knew his merits could not sufficiently admire him. Such fortune attended him, when, at the age of eighty, he went into Egypt to the aid of Tachos, and lay down with his men on the shore without any shelter, having merely such a couch that the ground was but covered with straw, and nothing more than a skin thrown upon it,183 while all his attendants lay in the same manner, in plain and well-worn attire, so that their equipments not only did not indicate that there was a king among them, but even raised a suspicion that he must be a man not very rich. The news of his arrival having reached the king's officers, presents of every kind were soon brought him; but when the officers inquired for Agesilaus, they could scarcely be made to believe that he was one of those who were sitting before them. When they presented him what they had brought, with a message from the king, he accepted nothing but some veal, and such sorts of meat as his present circumstances required; the ointments, chaplets, and sweetmeats he distributed among the slaves, and the other things he directed to be carried back. Upon this, the barbarians looked upon him still more contemptuously, thinking that he had made choice of what he had taken from ignorance of what was valuable.

As he was returning from Egypt, after having been presented by King Nectanabis 184 with two hundred and twenty talents, in order that he might bestow them upon his countrymen, and had arrived at what is called the harbour of Menelaus,185 lying between Cyrenae 186 and Egypt, he fell ill and died. His friends, in order the more conveniently to convey him to Sparta, enveloped his body, as they had no honey, in wax, and so carried it home.

XVIII. EUMENES.

Eumenes is secretary to Philip and Alexander, and afterwards commander in the cavalry, I.----After the death of Alexander he is allotted the province of Cappadocia, and is a steady friend to Perdiccas, II.----His proceedings on behalf of Perdiccas, III.----He defeats Craterus and Neoptolemus, IV.----Is pursued by Antigonus; his stratagems and escape, V.----His kindness to Olympias and Alexander's children, VI.----His continuance of hostilities against Antigonus; his device in his camp, VII.----He defeats Antigonus; is controlled by Alexander's veterans, VIII.----He eludes Antigonus by a stratagem, IX.----After again defeating Antigonus, he is betrayed by his own men, X.----In his confinement he longs to die, XI.----His death, XII.----After his death the officers of Alexander assume the title of kings; his funeral, XIII.

I. EUMENES was a native of Cardia.187 If success equal to his abilities had been granted him, he would not, indeed, have been a greater man (for we estimate great men by merit, not by fortune), but he would have been much more renowned, and more honoured. As he happened to live, however, in the days in which the Macedonians flourished, it was a great disadvantage to him residing among them, that he was of a foreign country. Nor was anything wanting to him but a noble descent; for, though he was of a family of distinction in his native city, the Macedonians were nevertheless dissatisfied that he should ever be preferred to them. They were obliged to submit, however, for he excelled them all in caution, vigilance, endurance, and acuteness and activity of intellect.

When he was but a youth, he was received into favour by Philip, the son of Amyntas, and after a short time was admitted into intimate friendship with him; for, even then, when he was so young, there appeared to be great natural talent in him. He therefore kept him near himself in the office of secretary, which is much more honourable 188 among the Greeks than among the Romans; for with us, secretaries are regarded as hirelings, as in reality they are; but with them, on the contrary, no one is admitted to that office who is not of good family and of known integrity and ability, because he must of necessity be the confidant of all their political measures. This post of confidence he held for seven years under Philip, and after Philip was assassinated, he was in the same office for thirteen years under Alexander. During the latter portion of this time, also, he commanded one of the two divisions of the cavalry called Hetaeriae.189 With both these princes he always had a place in the council, and was admitted to a knowledge of all their proceedings.

II. After the death of Alexander at Babylon, when kingdoms were allotted to each of his friends, and the superintendence of affairs was committed to the hands 190 of Perdiccas, to whom Alexander, when dying, had given his ring (a circumstance from which every one conjectured that Alexander had entrusted his kingdom to him, until his children should come of age to take the government upon themselves; 191 for Craterus and Antipater, who seemed to have the precedence of him, were absent, and Hephaestion, for whom Alexander, as might easily be perceived, had had the highest esteem, was dead), at that time Cappadocia was given to Eumenes, or rather appointed for him, for it was then in the power of the enemy. Perdiccas had sought with great eagerness to attach Eumenes to him, for he saw in him great honour and ability,192 and did not doubt that, if he could gain him over to his side, he would be of great assistance to him in the projects which he was meditating, since he purposed (what all in great power generally covet) to seize and secure for himself the shares of all the rest. Nor did he alone, indeed, entertain such designs, but all the others, who had been friends of Alexander, formed similar intentions. Leonnatus,193 in the first place, had resolved to seize upon Macedonia, and had endeavoured, by liberal promises, to prevail upon Eumenes to desert Perdiccas, and form an alliance with himself. Being unable to make any impression upon him, he attempted to take his life, and would have effected his purpose, had he not secretly escaped from his guards by night.

III. In the meantime those wars broke out, which, after the death of Alexander, were carried on to desperation;194 and all combined to ruin Perdiccas. Eumenes, though he saw that he was but weak, as he was obliged to stand alone against them all, yet did not forsake a friend, or show himself more desirous of safety than of honour. Perdiccas had set him over that part of Asia which lies between Mount Taurus and the Hellespont, and had opposed him alone to his European adversaries. 195 Perdiccas himself had marched against Ptolemy, to make an attack upon Egypt. Eumenes, as he had an army neither numerous nor strong, for it wanted exercise, and had not long been assembled, while Antipater and Craterus were said to be fast approaching, and to have passed the Hellespont, men who stood high in reputation and experience in war (and the Macedonian soldiers were then held in the same esteem in which the Romans are now held, for those have always been accounted the bravest who have attained the greatest power), Eumenes, I say, was aware, that if his troops should learn against whom they were being led, they would not only not proceed, but would disperse at the intelligence; and it was therefore a very clever stratagem of his, to lead his men through bye-roads, in which they could not hear the truth, and to make them believe that he was marching against some of the barbarians. In this artifice he successfully persevered, and drew out his army into the field, and joined battle, before the men were aware with whom, they were engaged. He succeeded, also, by an advantageous choice of ground, in fighting more with his cavalry, in which he had the superiority, than with his infantry, in which he was but weak.

IV. After they had continued the contest, with desperate efforts, through the greater part of the day, Craterus, the commander-in-chief, was killed, as well as Neoptolemus who held the second place in authority. With Eumenes Neoptolemus himself encountered, and as they grappled with one another, and fell from their horses to the ground (so that it might easily be seen that they fought with feelings of enmity, and warred more with their minds than with their bodies), they could not be separated till life left one of the two. Eumenes received some wounds from Neoptolemus, yet did not, on that account, retire from the field, but pressed more vigorously upon the enemy. The horse being routed, Craterus the general slain, and many, chiefly of high rank, being made prisoners, the infantry, as they were forced into a position from which they could not escape without the permission of Eumenes, begged peace of him. But when they had obtained it, they did not adhere to their word, but went off, as soon as they could, to Antipater. Eumenes endeavoured to save the life of Craterus, who was carried half dead from the field; but, not being able to succeed, he interred him, suitably to his dignity and their former friendship (for he had been intimate with him in Alexander's life-time), with a magnificent funeral, and sent his bones into Macedonia to his wife and children.

V. During the course of these proceedings on the Hellespont, Perdiccas was killed by Seleucus and Antigonus 196 on the river Nile, and the chief command was conferred upon Antipater. Upon this, those who had deserted him were condemned to death in their absence, the army giving their suffrage to that effect; and among those condemned was Eumenes, who, though he was affected at this blow,197 did not sink under it, or conduct the war with the less vigour.

But a course of necessitous circumstances, though they could not subdue the energy of his spirit, had yet some effect in diminishing it. Antigonus, however, who pursued him, was often, though he had plenty of all kinds of troops, severely harassed by him on the march, nor could he ever come to an engagement with him except in places in which a few could resist many. But at last, when he could not be taken by manoeuvring, he was hemmed in by numbers; still he extricated himself, though with the loss of several men, and took refuge in a fortress of Phrygia, called Nora; where, being besieged, and fearing that, by remaining in one place, he should lose his war-horses, as there was no room for exercising them, he adopted an ingenious expedient,198 by which the animal might be warmed and exercised standing, so that it might take its food more freely, and not be deprived of the benefit of bodily motion. He tied up its head 199 so high with a halter, that it could not quite touch the ground with its fore-feet; he then forced it, by lashing it behind, to leap up and throw back its heels; which motions excited perspiration no less than if the animal had run in an open course. Hence it happened (what was a matter of astonishment to all), that he led out his horses from the fortress, though he had been several months under siege, equally as sleek as if he had been keeping them in open fields. During that siege, as often as he desired, he either set on fire or demolished the works and defences of Antigonus. He, however, kept himself in that one place as long as the winter lasted; but, as the fortress could have no relief from without, and the spring was coming on, he pretended to be desirous of surrendering, and, while he was treating about the terms, eluded the officers of Antigonus, and brought himself and all his men off safe.

VI. When Olympias, who was the mother of Alexander, sent letters and messengers into Asia to Eumenes, to consult him whether she should proceed to re-possess herself of Macedonia (for she was then living in Epirus), and take upon herself the government there, he advised her, "above all things, not to stir, but to wait till Alexander's son should get the throne; yet, if she should be hurried into Macedonia by any irresistible longing, he recommended her to forget all injuries, and not to exercise too severe an authority over any one." But with neither of these suggestions did she comply; for she both went to Macedonia, and acted there with the greatest cruelty. She then entreated Eumenes, while he was still at a distance, "not to allow the bitterest enemies of Philip's house and family to extirpate his very race, but to give his support to the children of Alexander;" adding that, "if he would do her such a favour, he might raise troops as soon as possible, and bring them to her aid; and, in order that he might do so more easily, she had written to all the governors of the provinces that preserved their allegiance, to obey him, and follow his counsels." Eumenes, moved with this communication, thought it better, if fortune should so order it, to perish in showing his gratitude to those who had deserved well of him, than to live ungrateful.

VII. He therefore assembled troops, and prepared for war against Antigonus. But as there were with him several noble Macedonians, amongst whom were Peucestes, who had been one of Alexander's body-guard, and was then governor of Persia, and Antigenes, under whose command the Macedonian phalanx was, dreading envy (which, nevertheless, he could not escape), if he, being a foreigner, should have the chief authority rather than others of the Macedonians, of whom there was a great number there, he erected a pavilion at head quarters,200 in the name of Alexander, and caused a gold chair, with a sceptre and diadem, to be placed in it, directing that all should meet at it daily, that counsel might be taken there concerning matters of importance; for he thought that he should incur less envy if he appeared to manage the war under show of the authority, and with assumption of the name, of Alexander; and in this point he succeeded; for, as the meetings were held, not at the tent of Eumenes, but at that of the king, and measures concerted there, his superiority was in some degree concealed, though all was done by his agency alone.

VIII. He engaged with Antigonus in the country of the Paraetaci, not with his army in full array, but on the march, and forced him, after being severely handled, to return into Media to winter. He himself distributed his troops in winter-quarters through the neighbouring country of Persia, not as he chose, but as the will of his soldiers obliged him; for the phalanx of Alexander the Great, which had over-run Asia, and subdued the Persians, desired, in consequence of their established renown, and also through long-continued license, not to obey their officers but to command them, as our veterans now do. There is danger, therefore, lest ours should do what those did, and, by their insubordination and excessive licentiousness, ruin all, not less those whom they have supported than those whom they have opposed. And if any one reads the acts of those veterans, he will find the proceedings of ours like theirs, and be of opinion that there is no other difference between them but that of time. But I return to those of Macedonia. They had fixed upon their winter-quarters, not from regard to convenience for warfare, but for luxurious indulgence; and had separated into parties at a great distance from one another. Antigonus, hearing of their dispersion, and being aware that he was not a match for his enemies when prepared to receive him, resolved that some new plan must be adopted. There were two ways by which he might march from the country of the Medes, where he was wintering, to the winter-quarters of his adversaries, of which the shorter lay through desert tracts, which nobody inhabited by reason of the scarcity of water, but was only about ten days' march. The other, by which everybody travelled, presented a circuitous route of twice the length, but was well-supplied, and abounded with all necessaries. If he went by the latter, he felt sure that the enemy would know of his approach before he had accomplished the third part of the distance; but if he hurried through the deserts, he hoped that he might surprise his adversaries unawares. To effect his object, he ordered as many skins and sacks as possible to be got in readiness; and then forage and dressed provisions for ten days; desiring that as little fire as possible should be made in the camp. The route which he had in view he concealed from every one. Being thus provided, he set forward in the direction on which he had determined.

IX. He had accomplished about half the distance, when, from the smoke of his camp, a suspicion was hinted to Eumenes that an enemy was approaching. His officers held a meeting; and it was considered what ought to be done. They were all aware that their troops could not be assembled so soon as Antigonus seemed likely to be upon them; and, while they were all consequently in perplexity, and despairing of their safety,201 Eumenes said that "If they would but use activity, and execute his orders (which they had not done before), he would put an end to their difficulties; for, though the enemy might now finish his journey in five days, he would take care that they should be delayed not less than as many days more.202 They must therefore go about, and each collect his troops."

To retard the progress of Antigonus he adopted the following stratagem. He sent trustworthy men to the foot of the mountains, which lay over against the enemy's route, and ordered them, as soon as night came on, to make as large fires and as far dispersed, as they could; to reduce them at the second watch, and to make them very small at the third, and, by imitating the usages of a camp, to raise a suspicion in the enemy that there was actually a camp in those parts, and that intelligence had been given of their approach; and he told them to act in the same way on the following night. The men to whom this commission was given carefully observed their instructions. Antigonus, when darkness came on, saw the fires, and supposed that something had been heard of his coming, and that his enemies had assembled their force on that quarter. He therefore changed his intention, and, thinking that he could not surprise them unawares, altered his route, and took the longer circuit of the well-supplied road, on which he halted for one day, to refresh his weary men and recruit his horses, that he might come to battle with his army in better condition.

X. On this occasion Eumenes overreached a crafty general by stratagem, and obviated the suddenness of his attack; yet he gained but little by his success; for through the envy of the officers with whom he had to act, and the treachery of the Macedonian veterans, he was delivered up, after he had come off superior in the field, to Antigonus, though they had previously sworn, at three several times, that they would defend him and never forsake him. But such was the eagerness of some to detract from his merit, that they chose rather to break their faith than not betray him. Antigonus, however, though he had been a violent enemy to him, would have spared his life, if he had but been allowed to do so by his friends, because he was certain that he could not be better assisted by any one in those difficulties which, as was apparent to all, were likely to fall upon him. For Lysimachus, Seleucus, and Ptolemy, now powerful in resources, were assuming a threatening attitude, and he would be obliged to contend with them for supremacy. But those who were about him would not allow of such clemency; for they saw that if Eumenes were admitted to his councils, they themselves would be of small account in comparison with him. As for Antigonus himself, he had been so incensed against him, that he could never have been induced to relent, except by a strong expectation of eminent services from him.

XI. When he had committed him to custody, therefore, and the commander of the guard inquired how he would have him kept, he replied, "As the most furious lion, or the most savage elephant;" for he had not then determined whether he should spare his life or not. Meanwhile two classes of people crowded to gaze upon Eumenes, those who, from hatred of him, wished to feast their eyes 203 on his degradation and those who, from old friendship, desired to speak with him and console him. Many also came with them who were anxious to look at his person, and to see what sort of man he was whom they had feared so long and so much, and in whose destruction they had placed their hopes of victory. But Eumenes, when he had been some time under confinement, said to Onomarchus, in whose hands the chief command of the guard was, that "he wondered why he was thus kept a third day; for that it was not consistent with prudence on the part of Antigonus to treat 204 one whom he had conquered in such a manner, but that he should order him either to be put to death or released." As he seemed to Onomarchus to express himself somewhat arrogantly, he replied, "Why, if you were of such a spirit, did you not rather die on the field of battle, than fall into the hands of your enemy?" "Would indeed that that had befallen me," rejoined Eumenes, "but it did not happen because I never engaged with a stouter than myself; for I have never crossed swords with any one who did not yield to me; and I have not fallen by the prowess of my enemies, but by the perfidy of my friends." Nor was this assertion false; for he was a man not only of a graceful 205 and dignified bearing, but of strength sufficient for enduring fatigue; yet he was not so much distinguished for tallness of person as for handsomeness of shape.

XII. As Antigonus would not venture alone to determine concerning him, he referred the decision to a council; where, when almost all the officers, in great excitement, expressed their surprise that death had not been already inflicted on a man by whom they had been harassed so many years, so severely that they were often reduced to despair, a man who had cut off leaders of the greatest eminence; and in whom, though but a single individual, there was so much to be dreaded, that as long as he lived they could not think themselves safe, while, if he were put to death, they would have no further anxiety; and in conclusion they asked Antigonus, "if he gave Eumenes his life, what friends he would employ? for that they would not act under him with Eumenes." After thus learning the sentiments of the council, he nevertheless took time for consideration till the seventh day following; when, being afraid that a mutiny might break out in the army, he gave orders that no one should be admitted to Eumenes, and that his daily food should be withheld; for he said that "he would offer no personal violence to a man who had once been his friend." Eumenes, however, after suffering from hunger not more than three days, was killed by his guards on the removal of the camp, without Antigonus's knowledge.

XIII. Thus Eumenes, at the age of five-and-forty years, after having attended on Philip, as we have shown above, for seven years from the age of twenty, and having held the same office under Alexander for thirteen years, during one of which he had commanded a troop of cavalry; and after having, subsequently to Alexander's death, conducted armies as commander in-chief, and having sometimes repelled and sometimes cut off the most eminent generals, being made prisoner, not by the ability of Antigonus, but by the perjury of the Macedonians, ended his life in this manner.206 How great awe was entertained of him by all those who were styled kings after the death of Alexander the Great, may be easily judged from the following fact, that no one of them, while Eumenes lived, was called a king, but only a governor; but that, after his death, they at once assumed the regal dress and title; nor did they care to perform what they had originally promised, namely, to guard the throne for Alexander's children; but, as soon as the only defender of the children was removed, they disclosed what their real views were. In this iniquity the leaders were Antigonus, Ptolemy, Seleucus, Lysimachus, and Cassander.

Antigonus gave the dead body of Eumenes to his relations for burial; and they interred him with a military and magnificent funeral, and took care that his bones should he conveyed to Cappadocia to his mother, wife, and children.

XIX. PHOCION.

Phocion better known for his virtues than his military achievements, I.----In his old age he incurred the displeasure of his countrymen on various accounts, II.----Is exiled; his pleading before Philip; is sent back to Athens, III.----Is condemned at Athens, and put to death there, IV.

I. THOUGH Phocion the Athenian was often at the head of armies, and held the most important commands, yet the blamelessness of his life is much better known than his exertions in war. Of the one, accordingly, there is no recollection,207 but of the other the fame is great; and hence he was surnamed The Good. He was always poor, though he might have been extremely rich, by reason of the numerous offices conferred upon him, and the high commissions given him by the people. When he refused the present of a large sum of money from King Philip, and Philip's ambassadors urged him to receive it, and at the same time reminded him, that if he himself could easily do without it, he should nevertheless have some regard for his children, for whom it would be difficult, in the depth of poverty, to act up to the high character of their father, he gave them this answer: "If my children be like me, this same little farm, which has enabled me to reach my present eminence, will maintain them; but if they prove unlike me, I should not wish their luxury to be supported and increased at my expense."

II. After fortune had continued favourable to him almost to his eightieth year, he fell, towards the close of his life, into great unpopularity with his countrymen. In the first place, he had acted in concert with Demades in delivering up the city to Antipater; and, by his suggestions, Demosthenes and others, who were thought to deserve well of their country, had been sent into banishment by a decree of the people. Nor had he given offence only in this respect, that he had ill consulted the interest of his country, but also in not having observed the obligations of friendship; for though he had risen to the eminence which he then held through being supported and aided by Demosthenes, when he furnished him with means of defence against

Chares,208 and though he had several times come off with acquittal on trials, when he had to plead for his life, through having been defended by Demosthenes, he not only did not take the part of Demosthenes when he was in peril, but even betrayed him. But his fate was decided chiefly on one charge, that, when the supreme government of the state was in his hands, and he was warned by Dercyllus that Nicanor, the prefect of Cassander, was forming designs upon the Piraeeus, and Dercyllus begged him, at the same time, to take care that the city should not want provisions, Phocion told him in the hearing of the people, that there was no danger, and engaged to be security for the truth of his statement; whereas Nicanor, not long after, became master of the Piraeeus; and when the people assembled under arms to defend that harbour, without which Athens could not at all subsist, Phocion not only did not call any body to arms, but would not even take the command of those who were armed.

III. There were at that period in Athens two parties, one of which espoused the cause of the people, and the other that of the aristocracy; to the latter Phocion and Demetrius Phalereus were attached. Each of them relied on the support of the Macedonians; for the popular party favoured Polysperchon, and the aristocracy took the side of Cassander. After a time Cassander was driven from Macedonia by Polysperchon; and the people, in consequence, getting the superiority, immediately expelled from their country the leaders of the opposite faction, after they had been capitally convicted;209 and among them Phocion and Demetrius Phalereus; and they then sent a deputation on the subject to Polysperchon, to request him to confirm their decrees. Phocion went to him at the same time, and as soon as he arrived he was summoned to plead his cause, nominally before King Philip,210 but in reality before Polysperchon; for he at that time held the direction of the king's affairs. Being accused by Agnonides 211 of having betrayed the Piraeeus to Nicanor, and being thrown, by order of the council, into confinement, he was then conveyed to Athens, that a trial might there be held upon him according to law.

IV. On his arrival, as he was weak in his feet through age, and was brought to the city in a carriage, great crowds of people gathered about him, of whom some, calling to mind his former reputation, expressed commiseration for his declining years but the greater number were violently exasperated against him, from the suspicion that he had betrayed the Piraeeus, but especially because he had opposed the interest of the people in his old age. Hence not even the liberty of making a speech, and of pleading his cause, was granted him, but being forthwith sentenced to death, after some formalities of law had been despatched, he was delivered over to the eleven,212 to whom public criminals, by the custom of the Athenians, are wont to be consigned. As he was being led to execution, Emphyletus, a man with whom he had been very intimate, met him, and having exclaimed, with tears, "O what unworthy treatment you suffer, Phocion!" Phocion rejoined, "But not unexpected, for most of the famous men of Athens have come to this end." So violent was the hatred of the multitude towards him, that no free person dared to bury him; and he was accordingly interred by slaves

XX. TIMOLEON.

Timoleon delivers Corinth from the tyranny of his brother, and causes him to be put to death, I.----He expels Dionysius the younger from Sicily; defeats Hicetas; overcomes the

Carthaginians, II.----After settling affairs in Sicily, he lays down the government, III.----He loses his sight from old age, but still attends to the interests of his country; builds a temple to Fortune, IV.----Instances of his patience; his death, V.

I. TIMOLEON of Corinth was doubtless a great man in the opinion of everybody, since it happened to him alone (for I know not that it happened to any one else),213 to deliver his country, in which he was born, from the oppression of a tyrant, to banish a long established slavery from Syracuse (to the assistance of which he had been sent), and, on his arrival, to restore Sicily, which had been disturbed by war for many years, and harassed by barbarians,214 to its former condition. But in these undertakings he struggled not with one kind of fortune only, and, what is thought the more difficult, he bore good much more discreetly than evil fortune; for when his brother Timophanes, on being chosen general by the Corinthians, had made himself absolute by the aid of his mercenary troops, and Timoleon himself might have shared the sovereignty with him, he was so far from taking part in his guilt, that he preferred the liberty of his countrymen to the life of his brother, and thought it better to obey the laws of his country than to rule over his country. With this feeling, he contrived to have his brother the tyrant put to death by a certain augur, a man connected with them both, as their sister by the same parents 215 was married to him. He himself not only did not put his hand to the work, but would not even look upon his brother's blood; for, until the deed was done, he kept himself at a distance on the watch, lest any of his brother's guards should come to his aid. This most noble act of his was not equally approved by all; for some thought that natural affection had been violated by him, and endeavoured, from envy, to lessen the praise of his virtue. His mother, indeed, after this proceeding, would neither admit her son into her house, nor look upon him, but, uttering imprecations against him, called him a fratricide, and destitute of natural feeling. With this treatment he was so much affected, that he was sometimes inclined to put an end to his life, and withdraw himself by death from the sight of his ungrateful fellow-creatures.

II. In the meantime, after Dion was assassinated at Syracuse, Dionysius again became master of that city, and his enemies solicited assistance from the Corinthians, desiring a general whose services they might employ in war. Timoleon, being in consequence despatched thither, expelled Dionysius, with wonderful success, quite out of Sicily. Though he might have put him to death, he refused to do so, and secured him a safe passage to Corinth, because the Corinthians had often been supported by the aid of both the Dionysii, and he wished the memory of that kindness to be preserved, esteeming that victory noble, in which there was more clemency than cruelty; and, finally, he wished it not only to be heard, but seen, what a personage he had reduced from such a height of power to so low a condition. After the departure of Dionysius, he had to go to war with Hicetas, who had been the opponent of Dionysius; but that he did not disagree with him from hatred of tyranny, but from a desire for it, this was a sufficient proof, that after the expulsion of Dionysius he was unwilling to lay down his command. Timoleon, after defeating Hicetas, put to flight a vast army of the Carthaginians on the river Crimessus, and obliged those who had now for several years maintained their ground in Sicily, to be satisfied if they were allowed to retain Africa. He took prisoner also Mamercus, an Italian general, a man of great valour and influence, who had come into Italy to support the tyrants.

III. Having achieved these objects, and seeing not only the lands, but also the cities, deserted through the long continuance of the war, he assembled, in the first place, as many Sicilians as he could, and then sent for settlers also from Corinth, because it was by the Corinthians that Syracuse had been originally founded. He gave back to the old inhabitants their own lands, and divided such estates as had lost their owners in the war, among the new colonists; he repaired the dilapidated walls of the cities, and the neglected temples;216 he restored their laws and liberties to the several communities, and, after a most destructive war, established such tranquillity through the whole island, that he, and not those who had brought colonists thither at first, might have been thought the founder of those cities. The citadel of Syracuse, which Dionysius had built to overawe the city, he demolished to its foundations; other bulwarks of tyranny he removed, and exerted his efforts that as few traces as possible of servitude might be left.

Though he was possessed of so much influence that he might have ruled the Syracusans even against their will, and though he had so strongly gained the affection of all the Sicilians that he might have assumed supreme power without opposition from any one, he chose rather to be loved than to be feared. He therefore laid down his authority as soon as he could, and lived as a private person at Syracuse during the remainder of his life. Nor did he act in this respect injudiciously; for, what other rulers could scarcely effect by absolute power, he attained by the good will of the people. No honour was withheld from him; nor, when any public business was afterwards transacted at Syracuse, was a decision made upon it before Timoleon's opinion was ascertained. Not only was no man's advice ever preferred to his, but no man's was even compared to it; nor was this occasioned more by the good will of others towards him, than by his own prudence.

IV. When he was advanced in age he lost the sight of his eyes, without any apparent disease in them; a misfortune which he bore with so much patience, that neither did any one ever hear him complain, nor did he take a less part in private and public business. He used to come to the theatre,217 when any assembly of the people was held there, riding in a carriage by reason of his infirmity, and used to state from the vehicle what he thought proper. Nor did any one impute this to pride; for nothing arrogant or boastful ever came out of his mouth. Indeed when he heard his praises repeated, he never made any other observation than that "he paid and felt the utmost gratitude to the immortal gods for this favour, that when they had resolved on regenerating Sicily, they had appointed him, above all others, to be the leader to execute their will." For he thought that nothing in human affairs was done without the directing power of the gods; and he therefore erected a temple to Fortune 218 in his own house, and used to worship at it most religiously.

V. To this eminent virtue in his character were added certain wonderful incidents in his life; for he fought all his most remarkable battles on his birth-day; and hence it happened that all Sicily kept his birth-day as a festival. When one Lamestius, an impudent and ungrateful fellow, wanted to compel him to give bail for his appearance, as he said that he was merely dealing with him according to law, and several persons, flocking about him, would have curbed the insolence of the man by laying hands upon him, Timoleon entreated them all "not to do so, for that he had encountered extreme labours and dangers in order that Lamestius and others might enjoy such privileges; since this was the true form of liberty, if it were permitted to every one to try at law what he pleased." When a person, too, something like Lamestius, by name Demaenetus, had proceeded to detract from his actions before an assembly of the people, and uttered some invectives against Timoleon himself, he observed, that "he now enjoyed the fulfilment of his prayers,219 for that he had always made this his request to the immortal gods, that they would re-establish that degree of liberty among the Syracusans, in which it would be lawful for every man to say what he wished of any one with impunity." When he died, he was buried at the public expense by the Syracusans, in the Gymnasium, which is called the Timoleontean Gymnasium,220 all Sicily attending his funeral.

XXI. OF KINGS.

The Spartan kings, kings only in name; the most eminent kings of Persia, I.----The greatest kings of Macedonia; the only great sovereign of Sicily, II.----The kings that arose after the death of Alexander the Great, III.

I. THESE were almost all the generals of Greece 221 that seemed worthy of record, except kings, for we would not treat of them, because the actions of them all are narrated separately;222 nor are they indeed very numerous. As for Agesilaus the Lacedaemonian, he was a king in name, not in power, just like the other Spartan kings. But of those who were sovereigns with absolute authority, the most eminent were, as we think, Cyrus, king of the Persians, and Darius, the son of Hystaspes, both of whom, originally in a private station, obtained thrones by merit. The first of these was killed in battle among the Massagetae; Darius died a natural death at an advanced age. There are also three others of the same nation; Xerxes and the two Artaxerxes, Macrochir and Mnemon.223 The most remarkable act of Xerxes was, that he made war upon Greece, by land and sea, with the greatest armies in the memory of man. Macrochir is greatly celebrated for a most noble and handsome person, which he rendered still more remarkable by extraordinary bravery in the field; for no one of the Persians was more valorous in action than he. Mnemon was renowned for his justice; for, when he lost his wife through the wickedness of his mother, he indulged his resentment so far only, that filial duty overcame it.224 Of these, the two of the same name died a natural death; 225 the third was killed with the sword by Artabanus, one of his satraps.

II. Of the nation of the Macedonians, two kings far excelled the rest in renown for their achievements; Philip, the son of Amyntas, and Alexander the Great. One of these was cut off by a disease at Babylon; Philip was killed by Pausanias, near the theatre at Aegae, when he was going to see the games. Of Epirus, the only great king was Pyrrhus, who made war upon the people of Rome; he was killed by a blow from a stone, when he was besieging the city of Argos in the Peloponnesus. There was also one great sovereign of Sicily, Dionysius the elder; for he was both brave in action and skilful in military operations, and, what is not commonly found in a tyrant, was far from being sensual, or luxurious, or avaricious, and was covetous indeed of nothing but absolute and firmly-established sovereignty; and to attain that object he was cruel; for in his eagerness to secure it he spared the life of no one that he thought to be plotting against it. After having gained absolute power for himself by his abilities, he preserved it with remarkable good fortune, and died at the age of more than sixty, with his dominions in a flourishing condition. Nor in the course of so many years did he see the funeral of any one of his offspring, though he had children by three wives, and several grand-children had been born to him.

III. There arose also some great kings from among the followers of Alexander the Great, who assumed regal authority alter his death. Among these were Antigonus, and his son Demetrius, Lysimachus, Seleucus, and Ptolemy; of whom Antigonus was killed in battle, when he was fighting against Seleucus and Lysimachus; and Lysimachus was cut off in a similar way by Seleucus, for the alliance between the two being broken, they went to war with one another. Demetrius, after he had given his daughter to Seleucus in marriage, and yet the alliance between them could not be maintained the more faithfully on that account, was taken prisoner in battle, and died of some disease, the father-in-law in the custody of his son-in-law. Not long after, Seleucus was treacherously killed by Ptolemy Ceraunus, whom he had entertained, when he was expelled by his father from Alexandria, and stood in need of assistance from others. As for Ptolemy himself, he is said, after having resigned his throne to his son during his life, to have been deprived of life by that same son.

But, as we think that sufficient has been said concerning these, it seems proper not to omit Hamilcar and Hannibal, who, as is agreed, surpassed all the natives of Africa in power and subtilty of intellect.

XXII. HAMILCAR.

Hamilcar's success in Sicily; his defence of Eryx, and honourable capitulation, I.----His suppression of the rebellion raised by the Carthaginian mercenaries, II.----He takes his son Hannibal with him into Spain, and his son-in-law Hasdrubal, III.----Is killed in battle in Spain, IV.

I. HAMILCAR the Carthaginian, the son of Hannibal, and surnamed Barcas, began in the first Punic war, but towards the end of it, to hold the command of the army in Sicily; and though, before his coming, the efforts of the Carthaginians were unsuccessful both by sea and land, he, after he arrived, never gave way to the enemy,226 or afforded them any opportunity of doing him harm, but, on the contrary, often attacked the foe when occasion presented itself, and always came off with the advantage. Afterwards, though the Carthaginians had lost almost every place in Sicily, he so ably defended Eryx, 227 that there seemed to be no war going on there. In the meantime, the Carthaginians, having been defeated at sea, near the islands called Aegates,228 by Caius Lutatius, the Roman consul, resolved on putting an end to the war, and left the settlement of the matter to the judgment of Hamilcar, who, though he ardently desired to continue in arms, thought it, nevertheless, necessary to submit to make peace, because he saw that his country, exhausted by the expenses of the war, was no longer in a condition to bear the pressure of it; but such was his feeling on the occasion, that he soon meditated, if the affairs of his country should be but in a small degree improved, to resume the war, and to pursue the Romans with hostilities, until they should indisputably obtain the mastery, or, being conquered, should make submission. With this resolution he concluded a peace, but showed such a spirit in the transaction, that when Catulus refused to desist from hostilities unless Hamilcar, with such of his men as were in possession of Eryx, should lay down their arms and quit Sicily, Hamilcar replied, that, though his country submitted, he himself would rather perish on the spot than return home under such disgrace, for that it was not consistent with his spirit to resign to his enemies arms which he had received from his country as a defence against enemies.

II. Catulus yielded to his resolution. But Hamilcar, when he arrived at Carthage, found the republic in a far different condition than he had expected; for, through the long continuance of foreign troubles, so violent a rebellion had broken out at home, that Carthage was never in such danger, except when it was actually destroyed. In the first place, the mercenary troops, who had served against the Romans, and the number of whom amounted to twenty thousand, revolted; and these drew the whole of Africa over to their side, and laid siege to Carthage itself. With these disasters the Carthaginians were so much alarmed, that they requested aid even from the Romans, and obtained it. But at last, when they were almost sunk into despair, they made Hamilcar general, who not only repulsed the enemy from the walls of Carthage, though they amounted to a hundred thousand men in arms, but reduced them to such a condition, that being shut up in a confined space, they perished in greater numbers by famine than by the sword. All the towns that had revolted, and among them Utica and Hippo, the strongest cities of all Africa, he brought back to their allegiance to his country. Nor was he satisfied with these successes, but extended even the bounds of the Carthaginian empire, and re-established such tranquillity through all Africa, that there seemed to have been no war in it for many years.

III. These objects being executed according to his desire, he then, by dint of a spirit confident and incensed against the Romans, contrived, in order more easily to find a pretext for going to war with them, to be sent as commander-in-chief with an army into Spain, and took with him thither his son Hannibal, then nine years old. There also accompanied him a young man named Hasdrubal, a person of high birth and great beauty, who, as some said, was beloved by Hamilcar with less regard to his character than was becoming; for so great a man could not fail to have slanderers. Hence it happened that Hasdrubal was forbidden by the censor of public morals to associate with him; but Hamilcar then gave him his daughter in marriage, because, according to their usages, a son-in-law could not be interdicted the society of his father-in-law. We have inserted this notice of Hasdrubal, because, after Hamilcar was killed, he took the command of the army, and achieved great exploits; and he was also the first that corrupted the ancient manners of the Carthaginians by bribery. After his death Hannibal received the command from the army.

IV. Hamilcar, however, after he had crossed the sea, and arrived in Spain, executed some great undertakings with excellent success; he subdued some very powerful and warlike nations, and supplied all Africa with horses, arms, men, and money. But as he was meditating to carry the war into Italy, in the ninth year after his arrival in Spain, he was killed in a battle with the Vettones.

His constant hatred to the Romans seems to have been the chief cause of producing the second Punic war; for Hannibal, his son, was so wrought upon by the continual instigations of his father, that he would have chosen to die rather than not make trial of the Romans.

XXIII. HANNIBAL.

Hannibal, the greatest of generals, suffers from the envy of his countrymen, I.----Was the deadly enemy of the Romans, II.----He reduces Spain; besieges Saguntum; crosses the Alps, III.----His successful battles in Italy, IV.----His further proceedings in that country, V.----Is recalled to the defence of his country, and defeated by Scipio, VI.----Quits his country, and seeks refuge with Antiochus, VII.----Endeavours in vain to excite his countrymen to war; defeats the Rhodians, VIII.----Eludes the avarice of the Cretans, IX.----Stirs up Prusias against the Romans, X.----His stratagem in contending with Eumenes, XI.----Commits suicide to escape being delivered to the Romans, XII.----His attachment to literature, XIII.

I. HANNIBAL was the son of Hamilcar, and a native of Carthage. If it be true, as no one doubts, that the Roman people excelled all other nations in warlike merit, it is not to be disputed that Hannibal surpassed other commanders in ability as much as the Romans surpassed all other people in valour; for as often as he engaged with the Romans in Italy, he always came off with the advantage; and, had not his efforts been paralyzed by the envy of his countrymen at home, he would appear to have been capable of getting the mastery over the Romans. But the jealous opposition of many prevailed against the ability of one. He, however, so cherished in his mind the hatred which his father had borne the Romans, and which was left him, as it were, by bequest, that he laid down his life before he would abate it; for even when he was exiled from his country, and stood in need of support from others, he never ceased in thought to make war with the Romans.

II. To say nothing of Philip,[229] whom he rendered an enemy to the Romans, though at a distance from him, Antiochus was the most powerful of all kings at that period; and him he so inflamed with a desire for war, that he endeavoured to bring troops against Italy even from the Red Sea.[230] As some ambassadors from Rome were sent to that prince, in order to gain information respecting his intentions, and to endeavour, by underhand contrivances, to render Hannibal an object of suspicion to the king (as if, being bribed by them, he entertained other sentiments than before); and as they were not unsuccessful in their attempts, and Hannibal became aware of that fact, and found himself excluded from the privy council, he went at a time appointed to the king himself, and, after having said much concerning his attachment to him and his hatred to the Romans, he added the following statement: "My father Hamilcar," said he, "when I was a very little boy, being not more than nine years old, offered sacrifices at Carthage, when he was going as commander into Spain, to Jupiter, the best and greatest of the gods; and while this religious ceremony was being performed, he asked me whether I should like to go with him to the camp. As I willingly expressed my consent, and proceeded to beg him not to hesitate to take me, he replied, 'I will do so, if you will give me the promise which I ask of you.' At the same time he led me to the altar at which he had begun to sacrifice, and, sending the rest of the company away, required me, taking hold of the altar, to swear that I would never be in friendship with the Romans, This oath, thus taken before my father, I have so strictly kept even to this day, that no man ought to doubt but that I shall be of the same mind for the rest of my life. If, therefore, you entertain any friendly thoughts towards the Romans, you will not act imprudently if you conceal them from me; but whenever you prepare war, you will disappoint yourself unless you constitute me leader in it."

III. At this age, accordingly, he accompanied his father into Spain. After his father's death, when Hasdrubal was made general-in-chief, he had the command of all the cavalry. When Hasdrubal also was killed, the army conferred upon him the supreme command, and this act, when reported at Carthage, received public approbation.

Hannibal being thus made commander-in-chief, at the age of five-and-twenty, subdued in war, during the next three years, all the nations of Spain, took Saguntum, a city in alliance with the Romans, by storm, and collected three vast armies, of which he sent one into Africa, left another with his brother Hasdrubal in Spain, and took the third with him into Italy. He made his way through the forests of the Pyrenees,[231] he engaged, wherever he directed his course, with all the inhabitants of the country, and let none go unconquered. On arriving at the Alps, which separate Italy from Gaul, and which no one had ever crossed with an army before him, (except Hercules the Greek, from which achievement the forest there is now called the Grecian forest), he cut to pieces the people of the Alps who endeavoured to prevent his passage, laid open those parts, made roads, and put things in such a state, that an elephant fully equipped could walk where previously one unarmed man could scarcely crawl. Along this tract he led his army, and arrived in Italy.

IV. On the banks of the Rhone he engaged with the consul Publius Cornelius Scipio, and put him to flight. At the Po he fought with the same consul for the possession of Clastidium,[232] and expelled him from that place wounded and defeated The same Scipio, with his colleague Tiberius Longus, came against him a third time at the Trebia; he came to battle with them, and put both of them to flight. He then passed through the country of the Ligurians over the chain of the Apennnines, directing his course towards Etruria. During this march he was afflicted with so violent a distemper in his eyes, that he never had the use of his right eye so well afterwards. But even when he was troubled with this malady, and carried in a litter, he cut off Caius Flaminius the consul at the lake Trasimenus, being caught with his army in an ambush; and not long after he killed the praetor Caius Centenius, who was occupying the forest with a choice body of troops. He then proceeded into Apulia, where the two consuls, Caius Terentius Varro, and Paulus Aemilius, met him, both of whose armies he routed in one battle; the consul Paulus he killed, with several others of consular dignity, and among them Cnaeus Servilius Geminus, who had been consul the year before.

V. After fighting this battle, he marched towards Rome, nobody opposing him, and halted on the hills near the city. When he had lain encamped there some days, and was turning back towards Capua, Quintus Fabius Maximus, the Roman dictator, threw himself in his way in the Falernian territory. Here, though enclosed in a confined space, he extricated himself without any loss to his army. He deceived Fabius, a most skilful commander; for, when night had come on, he set fire to some bundles of twigs, tied upon the horns of oxen, and drove forward a vast number of those cattle, scattering themselves hither and thither. By presenting this object suddenly to their view,233 he struck such terror into the army of the Romans, that nobody ventured to stir beyond the rampart. Not many days after this success, he put to flight Marcus Minucius Rufus, master of the horse, who was equal in power with the dictator, and who had been drawn into an engagement by a stratagem. While he was at a distance, too, he cut off 234 Tiberius Sempronius Gracchus, consul for the second time, in the country of the Lucanians, after he had been inveigled into an ambush. In like manner he caused the death of Marcus Claudius Marcellus, consul for the fifth time, at Venusia. To enumerate his battles would occupy too much time; and this one observation, accordingly, (from which it will be understood how great a general he was), will be sufficient, that, as long as he continued in Italy, none made a stand against him in a regular engagement, none, after the battle of Cannae, pitched a camp against him in the field.

VI. Being recalled, without having suffered any defeat, to defend his country, he maintained a war with the son of that Publius Scipio whom he had routed first on the Rhone, again on the Po, and a third time on the Trebia. As the resources of his country were now exhausted, he wished, by a treaty with him, to put a stop to the war for a time, in order that he might engage in it afterwards with greater vigour. He came to a conference with him, but the conditions were not agreed upon. A few days after this meeting, he came to battle with Scipio at Zama; and being defeated (incredible to relate!) he made his way to Adrumetum, which is about three hundred miles 235 from Zama, in two days and two nights. In the course of his retreat, some Numidians, who had left the field in his company, formed a conspiracy against him; however he not only escaped them, but deprived them of life. At Adrumetum he assembled those who had survived the defeat, and, with the aid of new levies, drew together, in a few days, a numerous force.

VII. While he was most vigorously engaged in preparing for action, the Carthaginians made an end of the war by a treaty with the Romans. He had nevertheless afterwards the command of the army, and continued to act, as well as his brother Mago, in Africa, until the time when Publius Sulpicius and Caius Aurelius became consuls; for, during their term of office, ambassadors from Carthage went to Rome, to thank the Roman senate and people for having made peace with them, and to present them, on that account, with a crown of gold, requesting, at the same time, that their hostages might reside at Fregellae,236 and that their prisoners might be restored. An answer was made them, by a resolution of the senate, that "their present was acceptable and welcome, and that their hostages should live in the place which they desired, but that they would not restore the prisoners, because the Carthaginians retained Hannibal, by whose acts the war had been occasioned, and who was the bitterest of enemies to the name of Rome, in command of the army, as also his brother Mago." The Carthaginians, on hearing this answer, recalled Hannibal and Mago home. When he returned, he was made praetor, 237 in the two-and-twentieth year after he had been appointed king; 238 for, as consuls are elected at Rome, so, at Carthage, two kings are annually chosen, retaining their office for a year. In that post Hannibal conducted himself with the same activity as he had exhibited in war; for he took care, not only that there should be money raised from new taxes, to be paid to the Romans according to the treaty, but that there should be a surplus to be deposited in the treasury.

In the year after his praetorship, when Marcus Claudius and Lucius Furius were consuls, ambassadors from Rome came again to Carthage; and Hannibal, supposing that they were sent to demand that he should be delivered to the Romans, went secretly, before an audience of the senate was given them, on board a vessel, and fled into Syria to Antiochus. His departure being made public, the Carthaginians sent two ships to seize him, if they could overtake him. His property they confiscated; his house they razed to its foundations; and himself they declared an outlaw.

VIII. In the third year, however, after he had fled from home, and in the consulship of Lucius Cornelius and Quintus Minucius, Hannibal landed with five ships in Africa, on the coast of the Cyrenaeans, to try if he could move the Carthaginians to war, by giving them hope and confidence in Antiochus, whom he had now persuaded to proceed with his forces to Italy. Thither he summoned his brother Mago; and, when the Carthaginians knew of the circumstance, they inflicted on Mago the same penalties as they had laid on his absent brother. When they had let loose their vessels, and sailed off, in despair of success, Hannibal went to join Antiochus. Of Mago's end two accounts have been given; for some have left on record that he perished by shipwreck, others that he was killed by his own slaves.

Antiochus, if he had been as ready to obey Hannibal's advice in conducting the war as he had resolved to be when he undertook it, might have fought for the empire of the world nearer the Tiber than Thermopylae.239 Hannibal, however, though he saw him attempt many things imprudently, left him in nothing unsupported. He took the command of a few ships, which he had been directed to bring from Syria into Asia, and with these he engaged the fleet of the Rhodians in the Pamphylian sea,240 and though his men were overpowered in the struggle by the number of the enemy, he had the advantage himself in the wing in which he acted.

IX. After Antiochus was put to flight,241 Hannibal, fearing that he should be delivered to the Romans (an event which would doubtless have come to pass, if he had given the king an opportunity of securing him), went off to the people of Gortyn, in Crete, that he might there consider in what place he should settle himself. But, as he was the most perspicacious of all men, he saw that unless he took some precautions, he should be in great danger from the covetousness of the Cretans; for he carried with him a large sum of money, of which he knew that a report had gone abroad. He therefore adopted the following contrivance; he filled several pots with lead, covering the upper part with gold and silver, and deposited them, in the presence of the leading men 242, in the temple of Diana, pretending that he trusted his fortune to their honesty. Having thus deceived them, he filled the whole of some brazen statues, which he carried with him, with his money, and threw them down in an open place at his own residence. The Gortynians, meanwhile, guarded the temple with extreme care, not so much against others as against Hannibal himself, lest he should remove any thing without their knowledge, and carry it off with him.

X. The Carthaginian, having thus saved his property, and deceived all the Cretans, went into Pontus to Prusias, with whom he showed himself of the same mind as to Italy; for he did nothing but excite the king to arms, and animate him against the Romans, and seeing that he was not at all strong in domestic resources, he induced other princes to join him, and united warlike nations on his side. Eumenes, king of Pergamus, was at variance with Prusias, and war was maintained between them by sea and land, for which reason Hannibal was the more desirous that he should be crushed. Eumenes had the superiority on both elements, and Hannibal thought that, if he could but cut him off, his other projects would be easier of execution. To put an end to his life, therefore, he adopted the following stratagem. They were to engage by sea in a few days; Hannibal was inferior in number of vessels, and had to use art in the contest, as he was no match for his enemy in force. He accordingly ordered as many poisonous serpents as possible to be brought together alive, and to be put into earthen vessels, of which when he had collected a large number, he called the officers of his ships together, on the day on which he was going to fight at sea, and directed them all to make an attack upon the single ship of King Eumenes, and to be content with simply defending themselves against others, as they might easily do with the aid of the vast number of serpents; adding that he would take care they should know in what ship Eumenes sailed, and promising that, if they took or killed him, it should be of great advantage to them.

XI. After this exhortation was given to the soldiers, the fleets were brought out for action by both parties. When the line of each was formed, and before the signal was given for battle, Hannibal, in order to show his men where Eumenes was, despatched to him a letter-carrier in a boat with a herald's staff; who, when he reached the enemy's line of vessels, held out a letter, and signified that he was looking for the king; he was therefore immediately taken to Eumenes, because nobody doubted that there was something written in the letter relating to peace. The messenger, having thus made the king's ship known to his party, returned to the same place from which he had come. Eumenes, on opening the letter, found nothing in it but what was meant to ridicule him; and though he wondered as to the motive of it, and none could be discovered, yet he did not hesitate to come at once to battle. In the conflict, the Bithynians, according to the direction of Hannibal, fell all at once upon the ship of Eumenes. That prince, as he was unable to withstand their onset, sought safety in flight, but would not have found it, had he not taken refuge behind his guards, which had been posted on the neighbouring shore. As the rest of the Pergamenian ships bore hard upon the enemy, the earthen pots, of which we have previously spoken, began suddenly to be hurled into them. These, when thrown, at first excited laughter among the combatants, nor could it be conceived why such a thing was done, but when they saw their ships filled with serpents, and, startled at the strangeness of the occurrence, knew not what to avoid first, they put about their ships, and retreated to their camp upon the coast. Thus Hannibal, by his stratagem, prevailed over the force of the Pergamenians. Nor was this the only occasion; but often, at other times, he defeated the enemy with his troops on land, and with equally skilful management.

XII. While these transactions were taking place in Asia, it happened accidentally at Rome that certain ambassadors from Prusias took supper at the house of Lucius Quintius Flamininus, one of the consuls; and there, as mention was made of Hannibal, one of them observed that he was in the dominions of Prusias. This information Flamininus communicated the next day to the senate. The conscript fathers, who thought that they would never be free from plots as long as Hannibal was alive, sent ambassadors to Bithynia, and among them Flamininus, to request the king not to keep their bitterest enemy with him, but to deliver him up to them. To this embassy Prusias did not dare to give a refusal; he made some opposition, however, to one point, begging them not to require of him 243 what was contrary to the rights of hospitality, saying that they themselves might make Hannibal prisoner, if they could, as they would easily find out the place where he was. Hannibal indeed confined himself to one place, living in a fortress which had been given him by the king; and this he had so constructed that it had outlets on every side of the building, always fearing lest that should happen which eventually came to pass. When the Roman ambassadors had gone thither, and had surrounded his house with a number of men, a slave, looking out at a gate, told Hannibal that several armed men were to be seen, contrary to what was usual. Hannibal desired him to go round to all the gates of the castle, and bring him word immediately whether it was beset in the same way on all sides. The slave having soon reported how it was, and informed him, that all the passages were secured, he felt certain that it was no accidental occurrence, but that his person was menaced, and that his life was no longer to be preserved. That he might not part with it, however, at the pleasure of another, and dwelling on the remembrance of his past honours, he took poison, which he had been accustomed always to carry with him.

XIII. Thus this bravest of men, after having gone through many and various labours, found repose in the seventieth year of his age. Under what consuls he died, is not agreed; for Atticus has left it recorded in his chronicle that he ended his life in the consulship of Marcus Claudius Marcellus and Quintus Fabius Labeo; but Polybius says in that of Lucius Aemilius Paullus and Cnaeus Baebius Tamphilus; and Sulpicius in that of Publius Cornelius Cethegus and Marcus Baebius Tamphilus.

This great man, though occupied in such vast military operations, devoted some portion of his time to literature; for there are some books of his written in the Greek language, and amongst them one addressed to the Rhodians on the acts of Cnaeus Manlius Vulso in Asia.

Of the wars which he conducted many have given the history; and two of them were persons that were with him in the camp, and lived with him as long as fortune allowed, Silenus and Sosilus the Lacedaemonian; and this Sosilus Hannibal had as his instructor in the Greek language. But it is now time to make an end of this book, and to give an account of commanders among the Romans, that, when the actions of both are compared, it may be the better determined which generals deserve the preference.

XXIV. MARCUS PORCIUS CATO.

FROM THE SECOND BOOK OF CORNELIUS NEPOS.

Cato's birth, youth, and the offices that he held, I.----His consulship in Hither Spain; his severity as censor, II.----His eulogy; his studies and writings, III.

I. CATO,244 born in the municipal town of Tusculum,245 resided, when a very young man, and before he turned his attention to the attainment of office, in the territory of the Sabines, because he had an estate there which had been left him by his father. It was at the persuasion of Lucius Valerius Flaccus, whom he had for a colleague in his consulate and censorship, that he removed, as Marcus Perperna Censorius was accustomed to relate, to Rome, and proceeded to employ himself in the forum. He served his first campaign at the age of seventeen, in the consulship of Quintus Fabius Maximus and Marcus Claudius Marcellus. He was military tribune in Sicily. When he returned from thence, he attached himself to the staff of Caius Claudius Nero, and his service was thought of great value in the battle near Sena, in which Hasdrubal, the brother of Hannibal, fell. As quaestor, he happened to be under the consul, Publius Cornelius Scipio Africanus, with whom he did not live according to the intimate connexion of his office; for he was at variance with him during his whole life. He was made aedile of the commons 246 with Caius Helvius. As praetor he had the province of Sardinia, from which, when he was returning from Africa some time before in the character of quaestor, he had brought Quintus Ennius, the poet, an act which we value not less than the noblest triumph that Sardinia could have afforded.

II. He held the consulship with Lucius Valerius Flaccus, and had by lot Hither Spain for his province, from which he gained a triumph. As he stayed there a long time, Publius Scipio Africanus, when consul for the second time, wanted to remove him from his province, and to succeed him himself, but was unable, through the senate, to effect that object, even though he then possessed the greatest authority in the state; for the government was then conducted, not with regard for personal influence, but according to justice. Being displeased with the senate on this account, Scipio, after his consulship was ended, remained in the city as a private person.247

Cato, being made censor with the Flaccus above mentioned, exercised that office with severity; for he inflicted penalties on many noblemen, and introduced many new regulations into his edict,248 by means of which luxury, which was even then beginning to germinate, might be repressed. For about eighty years,249 from his youth to the end of his life, he never ceased to incur enmity in behalf of the commonwealth. Though attacked by many,250 he not only suffered no loss of character, but increased in reputation for virtue as long as he lived.

III. In all his pursuits he gave proofs of singular intelligence and industry; for he was a skilful agriculturist, well-informed in political affairs, experienced in the law, an eminent, commander, a respectable orator. He was also much devoted to literature, and though he had entered on the study of it at an advanced age, yet he made such progress in it, that you could not easily discover anything, either in Grecian or Italian history, that was unknown to him. From his youth he composed speeches. In his old age he began to write his Histories, of which there are ten books. The first contains the acts of the kings of Rome; the second and third show from whence each Italian state had its rise, for which reason he seems to have called the whole body of them Origines; in the fourth is related the first Carthaginian war; in the fifth the second; and all these subjects are treated in a summary way. Other wars he has narrated in a similar manner, down to the praetorship of Lucius Galba, who spoiled the Lusitanians. The leaders in these wars, however, he has not named, but has stated the facts without the names.

In the same books he has given an account of whatever seemed remarkable in Italy and Spain; and there are shown in them much labour and industry, and much learning.

Of his life and manners we have spoken more at large in the book which we wrote expressly concerning him at the request of Titus Pomponius Atticus; and we therefore refer those who would know Cato to that volume.

XXV. TITUS POMPONIUS ATTICUS.

Birth, talents, and education of Atticus, I.----He goes to Athens; assists the Athenians with money; his popularity there, II. III.----Is favourably regarded by Sulla; returns to Rome, IV.----Inherits property from Quintus Caecilius; his friendship with Cicero and Hortensius, V.----He abstains from, seeking offices or honours, but maintains his dignity of character, VI.----In the civil war he offends neither Pompey nor Caesar, VII.----After Caesar is killed, he supplies Brutus with money, VIII.----Is not even an enemy to Antony, whose wife and children he relieves, IX. ---- Antony's regard for the services of Atticus, X.----He aids many of the proscribed, XI.----He uses his interest only to avert dangers and troubles from his friends, XII.-----Of his private life; is a good father and citizen, XIII.----His meals; his prudence in pecuniary matters, XIV.----His love of truth and diligence, XV.----Agreeable to the old in his youth, and to the young in his old age, XVI.----His dutifulness to his mother, XVII.----His love of antiquity, and literature in general, XVIII.----His connexion with Caesar Octavianus, XIX.----His friendship with Caesar and Antony, XX.----His last illness, XXI.----He starves himself to death; his funeral, XXII.

I. TITUS POMPONIUS ATTICUS, descended from a most ancient Roman family,251 held the equestrian rank received in uninterrupted succession from his ancestors. He had a father who was active, indulgent, and, as times then were, wealthy, as well as eminently devoted to literature; and, as he loved learning himself, he instructed his son in all branches of knowledge with which youth ought to be made acquainted. In the boy, too, besides docility of disposition, there was great sweetness of voice, so that he not only imbibed rapidly what was taught him, but repeated it extremely well. He was in consequence distinguished among his companions in his boyhood, and shone forth with more lustre than his noble fellow-students could patiently bear; hence he stirred them all to new exertions by his application. In the number of them were Lucius Torquatus, Caius Marius the younger, and Marcus Cicero, whom he so attached to himself by his intercourse with them, that no one was ever more dear to them.

II. His father died at an early age. He himself, in his youth, on account of his connexion with Publius Sulpicius, who was killed when tribune of the people, was not unapprehensive of sharing in his danger; for Anicia, Pomponius's cousin, was married to Marcus Servius, the brother of Sulpicius. When he saw that the state, therefore, after the death of Sulpicius, was thrown into confusion by the disturbances of Cinna, and that no facility was allowed him of living suitably to his dignity without offending one side or the other (the feelings of the citizens being divided, as some favoured the party of Sulla and others that of Cinna) he thought it a proper time for devoting himself to his studies, and betook himself to Athens. He nevertheless, however, assisted young Marius, when declared an enemy, by such means as he could, and relieved him in his exile with money. And, lest his sojourn in a foreign country should cause any detriment to his estate, he transported thither a great portion of his fortune. Here he lived in such a manner, that he was deservedly much beloved by all the Athenians; for, in addition to his interest, which was great for so young a man, he relieved their public exigencies from his own property; since, when the government was obliged to borrow money,252 and had no fair offer of it, he always came to their aid, and in such a way, that he never received any interest of them, and never allowed them to be indebted to him longer than had been agreed upon; both which modes of acting were for their advantage, for he neither suffered their debt to grow old upon them, nor to be increased by an accumulation of interest. He enhanced this kindness also by other instances of liberality; for he presented the whole of the people with such a supply of corn, that seven modii 253 of wheat (a kind of measure which is called a medimnus at Athens) were allotted to each person.

III. He also conducted himself in such a way, that he appeared familiar with the lowest, though on a level with the highest. Hence it happened that they publicly bestowed upon him all the honours that they could, and offered to make him a citizen of Athens; an offer which he would not accept, because some are of opinion that the citizenship of Rome is forfeited by taking that of another city. As long as he was among them, he prevented any statue from being erected to him; but when absent, he could not hinder it; and they accordingly raised several statues both to him and Phidias,254 in the most sacred places, for, in their whole management of the state, they took him for their agent and adviser. It was the gift of fortune, then, in the first place, that he was born in that city, above all others, in which was the seat of the empire of the world, and had it not only for his native place but for his home; and, in the next, it was a proof of his wisdom, that when he betook himself to a city which excelled all others in antiquity, politeness, and learning, he became individually dear to it beyond other men.

IV. When Sulla arrived at Athens in his journey from Asia, he kept Pomponius in his company as long as he remained there, being charmed with the young man's politeness and knowledge; for he spoke Greek so well that he might have been thought to have been born at Athens; while there was such agreeableness in his Latin style, as to make it evident that the graces of it were natural, not acquired. He also recited verses, both in Greek and Latin, in so pleasing a manner that nothing could have been added to its attractions. It was in consequence of these accomplishments that Sulla would never suffer him to be out of his company, and wanted to take him away with him to Rome. But when he endeavoured to persuade him to go, "Do not desire, I entreat you," replied Pomponius, "to lead me with you against those, with whom, that I might not bear arms against you, I quitted Italy." Sulla, commending the good feeling of the young man, directed, at his departure, that all the presents which he had received at Athens should be carried to his house.

Though he resided at Athens many years, paying such attention to his property as a not unthrifty father of a family ought to pay, and devoting all the rest of his time either to literature or to the public affairs of the Athenians, he nevertheless afforded his services to his friends at Rome; for he used to come to their elections, and whatever important business of theirs was brought forward, he was never found wanting on the occasion. Thus he showed a singular fidelity to Cicero in all his perils; and presented him, when he was banished from his country, with the sum of two hundred and fifty sestertia.255 And when the affairs of the Romans became tranquil, he returned to Rome, in the consulship, as I believe, of Lucius Cotta and Lucius Torquatus; and the whole city of Athens observed the day of his departure in such a manner, that they testified by their tears the regret which they would afterwards feel for him.

V. He had an uncle, Quintus Caecilius, a Roman knight, an intimate friend of Lucius Lucullus, a rich man, but of a very morose temper, whose peevishness he bore so meekly, that he retained without interruption, to the extremity of old age, the good will of a person whom no one else could endure. In consequence, he reaped the fruit of his respectful conduct; for Caecilius, at his death, adopted him by his will, and made him heir to three-fourths of his estate, from which bequest he received about ten thousand sestertia.256

A sister of Atticus was married to Quintus Tullius Cicero; and Marcus Cicero had been the means of forming the connexion, a man with whom Atticus had lived in the closest intimacy from the time that they were fellow-students, in much greater intimacy, indeed, than with Quintus; whence it may be concluded that, in establishing friendship, similarity of manners has more influence than affinity. He was likewise so intimate with Quintus Hortensius, who, in those times, had the highest reputation for eloquence, that it could not be decided which of the two had the greater love for him, Cicero or Hortensius; and he succeeded in effecting what was most difficult, namely, that no enmity should occur between those between whom there was emulation for such eminence, and that he himself should be the bond of union between such great men.

VI. He conducted himself in such a manner in political affairs, that he always was, and always was thought to be, on the best side; 257 yet he did not mingle in civil tumults, because he thought that those who had plunged into them were not more under their own control than those who were tossed by the waves of the sea. He aimed at no offices (though they were open to him as well through his influence as through his high standing), since they could neither be sought in the ancient method, nor be gained without violating the laws in the midst of such unrestrained extravagance of bribery, nor be exercised for the good of the country without danger in so corrupt a state of the public morals. He never went to a public sale,258 nor ever became surety or farmer in any department of the public revenue.259 He accused no one, either in his own name or as a subscriber to an accusation.260 He never went to law about property of his own, nor was ever concerned in a trial. Offers of places, under several consuls and praetors, he received in such a way as never to follow any one into his province, being content with the honour, and not solicitous to make any addition to his property; for he would not even go into Asia with Quintus Cicero, when he might have held the office of legate under him; for he did not think it became him, after he had declined to take the praetorship,261 to become the attendant on a praetor. In such conduct he consulted not only his dignity but his quiet; since he avoided even the suspicion of evil practices. Hence it happened that attentions received from him 262 were more valued by all, as they saw that they were attributable to kindness, not to fear or hope.

VII. When he was about sixty years old, the civil war with Caesar broke out; but he availed himself of the privilege of his age, and went nowhere out of the city. Whatever was needful for his friends when going to Pompey, he supplied for them out of his own property. To Pompey himself, who was his intimate friend, he gave no offence; for he had accepted no distinction from him like others, who had gained honours or wealth by his means, and of whom some followed his camp most unwillingly, and some remained at home to his great disgust. But to Caesar the neutrality of Atticus was so pleasing, that when he became conqueror, and desired money from several private persons by letter, he not only forebore to trouble Atticus, but even released, at his request, his sister's son and Quintus Cicero from Pompey's camp. Thus, by adhering to his old course of life, he avoided new dangers.

VIII. Then followed the time, 263 when, on the assassination of Caesar, the commonwealth seemed to be in the hands of the Bruti 264 and Cassius, and the whole state turned towards them. Atticus, at that period, conducted himself towards Brutus in such a way, that that young man was not in more familiar intercourse with any one of his own age, than with him who was so advanced in years, and not only paid him the highest honour at the council, but also at his table. It was projected by some that a private fund should be formed by the Roman knights for the assassins of Caesar; a scheme which they thought might easily be accomplished if even only the leading men of that order would furnish contributions. Atticus was accordingly solicited by Caius Flavius, an intimate friend of Brutus, to consent to become a promoter of the plan. But Atticus, who thought that services were to be done to friends without regard to party, and had always kept himself aloof from such schemes, replied that, "If Brutus wished to make use of any of his property, he might avail himself of it as far as it would allow; but that about that project he would never confer or join with any man." Thus that combination of a party was broken by his dissent alone. Not long after, Antony began to get the advantage; so that Brutus and Cassius, despairing of their fortune, went into exile, into the provinces which had been given them for form's sake 265 by the consuls. Atticus, who had refused to contribute with others to that party when it was prosperous, sent to Brutus, when he was cast down and retiring from Italy, a hundred sestertia 266 as a present; and, when he was parted from him, he ordered three hundred 267 to be sent to him in Epirus. Thus he neither paid greater court to Antony when in power, nor deserted those that were in desperate circumstances.

IX. Next followed the war that was carried on at Mutina, 268 in which, if I were only to say that he was wise, I should say less of him than I ought; for he rather proved himself divine, if a constant goodness of nature, which is neither increased nor diminished by the events of fortune, may be called divinity. 269 Antony, being declared an enemy, had quitted Italy, nor was there any hope of bringing him back. Not only his open enemies, who were then very powerful and numerous, but also such as had lent themselves to the party opposed to him, and hoped to gain some share of praise 270 by doing him injury, persecuted his friends, sought to spoil his wife Fulvia of all her property, and endeavoured even to get his children put to death. Atticus, though he lived in intimate friendship with Cicero, and was very warmly attached to Brutus, yet would not only never give them his consent to act against Antony, but, on the contrary, protected, as much as he could, such of his friends as fled from the city, and supplied them with whatever they wanted. On Publius Volumnius, indeed, he conferred such obligations, that more could not have proceeded from a father. To Fulvia herself, too, when she was distracted with lawsuits, and troubled with great alarms, he gave his services with such constancy, that she never appeared to answer to bail 271 without the attendance of

Atticus. He was her surety in all cases, and even when she had bought an estate, in her prosperous circumstances, to be paid for by a certain day, and was unable after her reverse of fortune to borrow money to discharge the debt,272 he came to her aid, and lent her the money without interest, and without requiring any security for the repayment, thinking it the greatest gain to be found grateful and obliging, and to show, at the same time, that it was his practice to be a friend, not to fortune but to men; and when he acted in such a manner, no one could imagine that he acted for the sake of time-serving, for it entered into nobody's thoughts that Antony could regain his authority. But he gradually incurred blame from some of the nobles, because he did not seem to have sufficient hatred towards bad citizens.

X. Being under the guidance of his own judgment, however, he considered 273 rather what it was right for him to do, than what others would commend. On a sudden fortune was changed. When Antony returned into Italy, every one thought that Atticus would be in great peril, on account of his close intercourse with Cicero and Brutus. He accordingly withdrew from the forum on the approach of the leaders,274 from dread of the proscription, and lived in retirement at the house of Publius Volumnius, to whom, as we have said, he had not long before given assistance; (such were the vicissitudes of fortune in those days, that sometimes one party, and sometimes the other, was in the greatest exaltation or in the greatest peril;) and he had with him Quintus Gellius Canus, a man of the same age, and of a character very similar to his own; and this also may be given as an instance of the goodness of Atticus's disposition, that he lived in such close intimacy with him whom he had known when a boy at school, that their friendship increased even to the end of their lives. But Antony, though he was moved with such hatred towards Cicero, that he showed his enmity, not only to him, but to all his friends, and resolved to proscribe them, yet, at the instance of many, was mindful of the obliging conduct of Atticus; and, after ascertaining where he was, wrote to him with his own hand, that he need be under no apprehension, but might come to him immediately; as he had excepted him and Gellius Canus, for his sake, from the number of the proscribed; and that he might not fall into any danger, as the message was sent at night, he appointed him a guard. Thus Atticus, in a time of the greatest alarm, was able to save, not only himself, but him whom he held most dear; for he did not seek aid from any one for the sake of his own security only, but in conjunction with his friend; so that it might appear that he wished to endure no kind of fortune apart from him. But if a pilot is extolled with the greatest praise, who saves a ship from a tempest in the midst of a rocky sea, why should not his prudence be thought of the highest character, who arrives at safety through so many and so violent civil tumults?

XI. When he had delivered himself from these troubles, he had no other care than to assist as many persons as possible, by whatever means he could. When the common people, in consequence of the rewards offered by the triumvirs, were searching for the proscribed, no one went into Epirus 275 without finding a supply of everything; and to every one was given permission to reside there constantly. After the battle of Philippi, too, and the death of Caius Cassius and Marcus Brutus, he resolved on protecting Lucius Julius Mocilla, a man of praetorian rank, and his son, as well as Aulus Torquatus, and others involved in the same ill fortune, and caused supplies of everything to be sent them from Epirus to Samothrace.

To enumerate all such acts of his would be difficult; nor are they necessary to be particularized. One point we would wish to be understood, that his generosity was not timeserving or artful, as may be judged from the circumstances and period in which it was shown; for he did not make his court to the prosperous, but was always ready to succour the distressed. Servilia, for instance, the mother of Brutus, he treated with no less consideration after Brutus's death than when she was in the height of good fortune. Indulging his liberality in such a manner, he incurred no enmities, since he neither injured any one, nor was he, if he received any injury, more willing to resent than to forget it. Kindnesses that he received he kept in perpetual remembrance; but such as he himself conferred, he remembered only so long as he who had received them was grateful. He accordingly made it appear, to have been truly said, that "Every man's manners make his fortune." Yet he did not study his fortune 276 before he formed himself, taking care that he might not justly suffer for any part of his conduct.

XII. By such conduct, therefore, he brought it to pass, that Marcus Vipsanius Agrippa, who was united in the closest intimacy with young Caesar, though, through his own interest and Caesar's influence, he had power to choose a wife from any rank whatever, fixed on a connexion with him rather than with any other, and preferred a marriage with the daughter of a Roman knight to an alliance with the most noble of women. The promoter of this match (for it is not to be concealed) was Mark Antony, when triumvir for settling the state; but though Atticus might have increased his property by the interest of Antony, he was so far from coveting money, that he never made use of that interest except to save his friends from danger or trouble;277 a fact which was eminently remarkable at the time of the proscription; for when the triumviri, according to the way in which things were then managed, had sold the property of Lucius Saufeius, a Roman knight, who was of the same age as Atticus, and who, induced by a love for the study of philosophy, had lived with him several years at Athens, and had valuable estates in Italy, it was effected by the efforts and perseverance of Atticus, that Saufeius was made acquainted by the same messenger, that "he had lost his property and had recovered it." He also brought off Lucius Julius Calidus, whom I think I may truly assert to have been the most elegant poet that our age has produced since the death of Lucretius and Catullus, as well as a man of high character, and distinguished by the best intellectual accomplishments, who, in his absence, after the proscription of the knights, had been enrolled in the number of the proscribed by Publius Volumnius, the captain of Antony's engineers, on account of his great possessions in Africa; an act on the part of Atticus, of which it was hard to judge at the time, whether it were more onerous or honourable. But it was well known that the friends of Atticus, in times of danger, were not less his care in their absence than when they were present.

XIII. Nor was he considered less deserving as a master of a family than as a member of the state; for though he was very rich, no man was less addicted to buying or building than he. Yet he lived in very good style, and had everything of the best; for he occupied the house that had belonged to Tamphilus 278 on the Quirinal hill, which was bequeathed to him by his uncle, and the attractions of which consisted, not in the building itself, but in the wood by which it was surrounded; for the edifice, constructed after the ancient fashion, showed more regard to convenience 279 than expense, and Atticus made no alteration in it except such as he was obliged to make by the effects of time. He kept an establishment of slaves of the best kind, if we were to judge of it by its utility, but if by its external show, scarcely coming up to mediocrity; for there were in it well-taught youths, excellent readers, and numerous transcribers of books, insomuch that there was not even a footman 280 that could not act in either of those capacities extremely well. Other kinds of artificers,281 also, such as domestic necessities require, were very good there, yet he had no one among them that was not born and instructed in his house; all which particulars are proofs, not only of his self-restraint, but of his attention to his affairs; for not to desire inordinately what he sees desired by many, gives proof of a man's moderation; and to procure what he requires by labour rather than by purchase, manifests no small exertion. Atticus was elegant, not magnificent; polished, not extravagant; he studied, with all possible care, neatness, and not profusion. His household furniture was moderate, not superabundant, but so that it could not be considered as remarkable in either respect. Nor will I omit the following particular, though I may suppose that it will be unimportant to some: that though he was a hospitable Roman knight, and invited, with no want of liberality, men of all ranks to his house, we know that he was accustomed to reckon from his day-book, as laid out in current expenses, not more than three thousand asses 282 a month, one month with another; and we relate this, not as hearsay, but as what we know, for we were often present, by reason of the intimacy between us, at his domestic arrangements.

XIV. At his banquets no one ever heard any other entertainment for the ears 283 than a reader; an entertainment which we, for our parts, think in the highest degree pleasing; nor was there ever a supper at his house without reading of some kind, that the guests might find their intellect gratified no less than their appetite, for he used to invite people whose tastes were not at variance with his own. After a large addition, too, was made to his property, he made no change in his daily arrangements, or usual way of life, and exhibited such moderation, that he neither lived unhandsomely, with a fortune of two thousand sestertia,284 which he had inherited from his father, nor did he, when he had a fortune of a hundred thousand sestertia,285 adopt a more splendid mode of living than that with which he had commenced, but kept himself at an equal elevation in both states. He had no gardens, no expensive suburban or maritime villa, nor any farm except those at Ardea and Nomentum; and his whole revenue arose from his property in Epirus and at Rome. Hence it may be seen that he was accustomed to estimate the worth of money, not by the quantity of it, but by the mode in which it was used.

XV. He would neither utter a falsehood himself, nor could he endure it in others. His courtesies, accordingly, were paid with a strict regard to veracity, just as his gravity was mingled with affability; so that it is hard to determine whether his friends' reverence or love for him were the greater. Whatever he was asked to do, he did not promise without solemnity,286 for he thought it the part, not of a liberal, but of a light-minded man, to promise what he would be unable to perform. But in striving to effect what he had once engaged to do, he used to take so much pains, that he seemed to be engaged, not in an affair entrusted to him, but in his own. Of a matter which he had once taken in hand, he was never weary; for he thought his reputation, than which he held nothing more dear, concerned in the accomplishment of it. Hence it happened that he managed all the commissions 287 of the Ciceros, Cato, Marius, Quintus Hortensius, Aulus Torquatus, and of many Roman knights besides. It may therefore be thought certain that he declined business of state, not from indolence, but from judgment.

XVI. Of his kindness of disposition, I can give no greater proof than that, when he was young, he was greatly liked by Sulla, who was then old, and when he was old, he was much beloved by Marcus Brutus, then but young; and that with those friends of the same age as himself, Quintus Hortensius and Marcus Cicero, he lived in such a manner that it is hard to determine to which age his disposition was best adapted, though Marcus Cicero loved him above all men, so that not even his brother Quintus was dearer or more closely united to him. In testimony of this fact (besides the books in which Cicero mentions him, and which have been published to the world), there are sixteen books of letters, written to Atticus, which extend from his consulship to his latter days, and which he that reads will not much require a regular history of those times; for all particulars concerning the inclinations of leading men, the faults of the generals, and the revolutions in the government, are so fully stated in them that every thing is made clear; and it may be easily concluded that wisdom is in some degree divination, as Cicero not only predicted that those things would happen which took place during his life, but foretold, like a prophet, the things which are coming to pass at present

XVII. Of the affectionate disposition of Atticus towards his relatives, why should I say much, since I myself heard him proudly assert, and with truth, at the funeral of his mother, whom he buried at the age of ninety, that "he had never had occasion to be reconciled to his mother," 288 and that "he had never been at all at variance with his sister," who was nearly of the same age with himself; a proof that either no cause of complaint had happened between them, or that he was a person of such kind feelings towards his relatives, as to think it an impiety to be offended with those whom he ought to love. Nor did he act thus from nature alone, though we all obey her, but from knowledge; for he had fixed in his mind the precepts of the greatest philosophers, so as to use them for the direction of his life, and not merely for ostentation.

XVIII. He was also a strict imitator of the customs of our ancestors, and a lover of antiquity, of which he had so exact a knowledge, that he has illustrated it throughout in the book in which he has characterized 289 the Roman magistrates; for there is no law, or peace, or war, or illustrious action of the Roman people, which is not recorded in it at its proper period, and, what was extremely difficult, he has so interwoven in it the origin of families, that we may ascertain from it the pedigrees of eminent men. He has given similar accounts too, separately, in other books; as, at the request of Marcus Brutus, he specified in order the members of the Junian family, from its origin to the present age, stating who each was, from whom sprung, what offices he held, and at what time. In like manner, at the request of Marcellus Claudius, he gave an account of the family of the Marcelli; at the request of Scipio Cornelius and Fabius Maximus, of that of the Fabii and Aemilii; than which books nothing can be more agreeable to those who have any desire for a knowledge of the actions of illustrious men.

He attempted also poetry, in order, we suppose, that he might not be without experience of the pleasure of writing it; for he has characterized in verse such men as excelled the rest of the Roman people in honour and the greatness of their achievements, so that he has narrated, under each of their effigies, their actions and offices, in not more than four or five lines; and it is almost inconceivable that such important matters could have been told in so small a space. There is also a book of his written in Greek, on the consulship of Cicero.

These particulars, so far, were published by me whilst Atticus was alive.

XIX. Since fortune has chosen that we should outlive him, we will now proceed with the sequel, and will show our readers by example, as far as we can, that (as we have intimated above) "it is in general a man's manners that bring him his fortune."290 For Atticus, though content in the equestrian rank in which he was born, became united by marriage with the emperor Julius's son, whose friendship he had previously obtained by nothing else but his elegant mode of living, by which he had charmed also other eminent men in the state, of equal birth,291 but of lower fortune; for such prosperity attended Caesar, that fortune gave him everything that she had previously bestowed upon any one, and secured for him what no citizen of Rome had ever been able to attain. Atticus had a granddaughter, the daughter of Agrippa, to whom he had married his daughter in her maidenhood; and Caesar betrothed her, when she was scarcely a year old, to Tiberius Claudius Nero, son of Drusilla, and step-son to himself; an alliance which established their friendship, and rendered their intercourse more frequent.

XX. Even before this connexion, however, Caesar not only, when he was absent from the city, never despatched letters to any one of his friends without writing to Atticus what he was doing, what, above all, he was reading, in what place he was, and how long he was going to stay in it, but even when he was in Rome, and through his numberless occupations enjoyed the society of Atticus less frequently than he wished, scarcely any day passed in which he did not write to him, sometimes asking him something relating to antiquity, sometimes proposing to him some poetical question, and sometimes, by a jest, drawing from him a longer letter than ordinary. Hence it was, that when the temple of Jupiter Feretrius, built in the Capitol by Romulus, was unroofed and falling down through age and neglect, Caesar, on the suggestion of Atticus, took care that it should be repaired.

Nor was he less frequently, when absent, addressed in letters by Mark Antony; so that, from the remotest parts of the earth, he gave Atticus precise information what he was doing, and what cares he had upon him. How strong such attachment is, he will be easily able to judge, who can understand how much prudence is required to preserve the friendship and favour of those between whom there existed not only emulation in the highest matters, but such a mutual struggle to lessen one another as was sure to happen between Caesar and Antony, when each of them desired to be chief, not merely of the city of Rome, but of the whole world.

XXI. After he had completed, in such a course of life, seventy-seven years, and had advanced, not less in dignity, than in favour and fortune (for he obtained many legacies on no other account than his goodness of disposition), and had also been in the enjoyment of so happy a state of health, that he had wanted no medicine for thirty years, he contracted a disorder of which at first both himself and the physicians thought lightly, for they supposed it to be a tenesmus, and speedy and easy remedies were proposed for it; but after he had passed three months under it without any pain, except what he suffered from the means adopted for his cure, such force of the disease fell into the one intestine,292 that at last a putrid ulcer broke out through his loins. Before this took place, and when he found that the pain was daily increasing, and that fever was superadded, he caused his son-in-law Agrippa to be called to him, and with him Lucius Cornélius Balbus and Sextus Peducaeus. When he saw that they were come, he said, as he supported himself on his elbow, "How much care and diligence I have employed to restore my health on this occasion, there is no necessity for me to state at large, since I have yourselves as witnesses; and since I have, as I hope, satisfied you, that I have left nothing undone that seemed likely to cure me, it remains that I consult for myself. Of this feeling on my part I had no wish that you should be ignorant; for I have determined on ceasing to feed the disease; as, by the food and drink that I have taken during the last few days, I have prolonged life only so as to increase my pains without hope of recovery. I therefore entreat you, in the first place, to give your approbation to my resolution, and in the next, not to labour in vain by endeavouring to dissuade me from executing it."

XXII. Having delivered this address with so much steadiness of voice and countenance, that he seemed to be removing, not out of life, but out of one house into another,----when Agrippa, weeping over him and kissing him, entreated and conjured him "not to accelerate that which nature herself would bring, and, since he might live some time longer,293 to preserve his life for himself and his friends,"----he put a stop to his prayers, by an obstinate silence. After he had accordingly abstained from food for two days, the fever suddenly left him, and the disease began to be less oppressive. He persisted, nevertheless, in executing his purpose; and in consequence, on the fifth day after he had fixed his resolution, and on the last day of February, in the consulship of Cnaeus Domitius and Caius Sosius, he died.294 His body was carried out of his house on a small couch, as he himself had directed, without any funereal pomp, all the respectable portion of the people attending, 295 and a vast crowd of the populace. He was buried close by the Appian way, at the fifth milestone from the city, in the sepulchre of his uncle Quintus Caecilius.

FRAGMENTS 296

I. Words excerpted from the letter of Cornelia, mother of the Gracchi, from the book of Cornelius Nepos On the Latin Historians.297

You will say that it is beautiful to take revenge on enemies. That seems neither greater nor more beautiful to anyone than to me, but <only> if it is allowed by the safety of the republic to pursue it. But inasmuch as that cannot be done, for a long time and in many ways our enemies will not perish, as this is better than that the republic be overthrown and perish.

II. Likewise from another place.

I intend to swear formally that, apart from those who killed Tiberius Gracchus, no enemy has caused me so many troubles and so many labours as you on account of these things; you who should, as the only one <surviving> of all those children whom I had previously, have taken trouble and care that I should have the fewest anxieties in my old age; certainly you should have wished that all your actions should be pleasing to me and to consider it a sin to do things of great importance against my advice, especially when a small part of life remains to me.

Cannot even that brief span aid me in preventing you from opposing me and ruining the republic? Finally what end will there be? Will our family ever stop the insanity? Will it ever be possible to have moderation? Will we ever desist from causing and suffering trouble? Will we ever be embarrassed to confuse and disturb the republic? But if it is not possible in any way, when I am dead, campaign for the tribunacy; do whatever you like, as far as I am concerned, when I am no longer aware of it. When I am dead, you will make sacrifices at my tomb, and invoke the parental deity. In that time, will you not be ashamed to ask for the prayers of those as gods whom living and present you abandoned and deserted? Jupiter forbid you to persist in that, or allow such madness to come into your soul. And if you persist, I fear that you will receive so much trouble in your whole life that it will never be possible to make peace with yourself.

III. Cornelius Nepos, in the book On the Latin Historians, in praise of Cicero.298

You should not ignore that this 299 is the sole branch of Latin letters that still cannot be compared with that of the Greeks, but was left rude and inchoate by the death of Cicero. For he was the only man who could or sought to produce history in a worthy way, since he highly polished up the rude eloquence handed down from the great men of the past, and strengthened Latin philosophy, before him uncouth, with his style. From which I doubt whether from his loss the republic or history suffered more.

IV. Likewise.

Opulent and divine nature, to obtain greater admiration and wider benefit, has chosen not to give every gift to one man, nor further to deny every gift to anyone.

V. Cornelius Nepos so wrote to ... Cicero. 300

I am so far from thinking that philosophy teaches how to live, and the thing that perfects a blessed life, that I consider no men have more need of teachers in how to live than most of those who spend their time teaching it. For I see that a great part of those who lecture most subtly in the schools on decency and continence themselves live in lusts for every kind of sensual pleasure.

CHRONOLOGICAL SUMMARY OF EVENTS MENTIONED BY CORNELIUS NEPOS.

In this Chronological Summary such events only are noticed as more immediately concern Cornelius Nepos. Facts that are not found here may be sought in the Chronology appended to Justin in this volume, or in general Chronological Tables. The dates are taken from Tzschucke.

B.C.

512. Miltiades sent to the Chersones. Milt. 1

507. -----------returns to Athens. Milt 3.

489. -----------dies. Milt. 7.

483. Aristides banished. Arist. 1.

----Themistocles begins to construct the harbour of the Piraeeus.

479 ----------------prevails on the Athenians to rebuild the walls of their city. Them. 6.

477. --------------- completes the Piraeeus. Them. 6.

----Pausanias sails to Cyprus with the combined fleet of Greece. Paus. 2.

---- Aristides establishes the treasury of Greece at Delos. Arist. 3.

471. Themistocles flees to Artaxerxes. Them. 8.

467. Death of Aristides. Arist. 3.

466. ---- -----, Themistocles. Them. 10.

463. Cimon subdues the Thasians. Cim 2.

460. -------banished. Cim. 3.

455. -------recalled. Ib.

450.-------defeats the Persians in Cyprus. Ib.

449. -------dies in Cyprus. Ib.

416. Alcibiades, with Nicias and Lamachus, sails against Syracuse. Alcib. 3.

415. -------------, accused of treachery to his country, flees to Sparta. Alcib. 4.

414.-------------prevails on the Lacedaemonians to fortify Decelia. Ib.

411. -------------joins the Athenian army; is united in command with Thrasybulus and Theramenes; defeats the Lacedaemonians. Alcib. 5.

408.-------------is unsuccessful, and banished. Alcib. 6, 7.

406. Dionysius the elder becomes tyrant of Syracuse. Dion. 1; De Reg. 2.

405. Lysander terminates the Peloponnesian war. Lys. 1; Alcib. 8; Conon 1

404. Alcibiades killed, Alcib. 10.

403. Lysander tried for attempting to bribe the oracle of Jupiter Ammon. Lys. 3.

401. Thrasybulus overthrows the Thirty Tyrants. Thras. 1.

400. Agesilaus becomes king of Sparta. Ages. 1.

398. Plato goes to Syracuse. Dion 2.

396. Lysander falls in battle against the Thebans at Haliartus. Lys, 3.

395. Conon defeats Pisander at Cnidus. Con. 4.

394. --------, with the aid of the Thebans, rebuilds the walls of Athens, Con. 4, 5.

---- ---------is made prisoner by Tiribazus at Sardis. Ib.

393 Iphicrates defeats the Spartans at Corinth. Iph. 2.

390. Thrasybulus killed at Aspendus. Thras 4.

387. Chabrias subdues Cyprus. Chab. 2.

385. Datames made governor of Cilicia by Artaxerxes. Dat. 1.

382. Phoebidas seizes on the citadel of Thebes. Pelop. 1.

378. The Theban exiles retake it. Pelop. 3.

377. Agesilaus invades Boeotia; is withstood by Chabrias. Chab. 1.

---- Chabrias assists Acoris king of Egypt. Chab. 3.

---- Iphicrates goes to the assistance of Artaxerxes. Iph. 2.

376. Timotheus defeats the Lacedaemonians at Leucate. Tim. 2.

374. Iphicrates returns to Athens. Iph. 2.

371. Epaminondas defeats the Spartans at Leuctra. Epam. 8

370. Iphicrates protects Eurydice of Macedonia. Iph. 3.

369. Epaminoudas invades Laconia, advances on Sparta, and restores Messene. Epam. 7. 8.

---- ------------------and Pelopidas support the Arcadians in their struggle with the Spartans. Pelop. 4.

---- Iphicrates assists the Lacedaemonians. Iph. 2.

388. Pelopidas imprisoned by Alexander of Pherae. Pelop. 5.

------------------rescued by Epaminondas. Ib.

386. Epaminondas at war in the Peloponnesus. Epam. 7.

334. Pelopidas killed in a battle with Alexander of Pherae. Pelop. 5.

----Timotheus at war with the Olynthians Tim. 1.

363. Epaminoudas falls victorious at Mantinea. Epam. 9.

332. Death of Agesilaus. Ages. 8.

---- Datames revolts from Artaxerxes. Dat.

358. Death of Chabrias. Chab. 4.

----Dion flees from Dionysius, and prepares to go to war with him. Dion. 4.

357. ------takes possession of Syracuse. Dion. 5.

356. The Athenians, under Chares, Iphicrates, and Timotheus, at war with their allies. Tim. 3.

----- Timotheus fined by the Athenians. Tim. 3.

355. Dion assassinated at Syracuse. Dion 9; Timol. 2.

345. Expedition of Timoleon to Syracuse; he gives liberty to the Syracusans. Ib.

344 Timoleon expels Dionysius, who goes to Corinth. Ib.

342. Timoleon re-establishes a republican form of government at Syracuse; secures peace to all Sicily. Ib.

337. -----------dies. Timol. 4.

322. Phocion procures for Athens the protection of Antipater. Phoc. 2.

321. Eumenes defeats Craterus and Neoptolemus. Eum. 3, 4.

-----------------besieged by Antigonus at Nora. Eum. 5.

318. Nicanor, at the command of Cassander, takes possession of the Piraeeus. Phoc. 2.

----Death of Phocion. Phoc. 4.

317. Eumenes commences hostilities against Antigonus. Eum. 7.

316. -----------taken and put to death by Antigonus. Eum. 10-12.

301. Antigonus killed at Ipsus. De Reg. 3.

272. Pyrrhus killed at Argos. De Reg. 2.

248. Hamilcar made commander of the Punic fleet. Hamil. 1.

238. -----------sent as commander-in-chief into Spain. Hamil. 3; Hann. 2.

229. -----------'s death. Ham. 3.

221. Hannibal becomes commander-in-chief in Spain. Hamil. 3; Hann. 3.

214. Cato military tribune. Cat. 1.

205. ------quaestor to Publius Scipio. 76.

198. ------praetor, with Sardinia for his province. Cat. 1.

195. ------made consul with Lucius Valerius Flaccus. Cat. 1, 2.

194. ------obtains a triumph for his successes in Spain. Cat. 2.

184. ------Censor with L. Flaccus. Cat. 2.

149. ------dies at the age of 85. Cat. 2.

109. Birth of Pomponius Atticus.

88. Publius Sulpicius, tribune of the people, killed by Sulla. Att. 2,

87. Atticus retires to Athens. Ib.

84. Sulla visits Athens in his return from Asia. Att. 4.

65. Atticus returns to Rome. Ib.

32. Death of Atticus. Att 22.

[Footnotes numbered and moved to the end]

1. * Plerosque.] For plurimos. So, a little below, pleraque----sunt decora, for plurima.

2. † Hoc genus scripturæ.] These brief memoirs of eminent men, interspersed with allusions to national habits and peculiarities.

3. ‡ Tibiis cantasse.] The plural, flutes, is used, because the Greeks, and the Romans, who adopted the practice from them, played on different kinds of flutes or pipes, equal and unequal, right and left-handed, and often on two at once. See Colman's preface to his translation of Terence; Smith's Classical Dict. art. Tibia; Life of Epaminondas, c. 2.

4. § Sororem germanam.] A half-sister by the mother's side was called soror uterina. Her name was Elpinice. See the Life of Cimon.

5. * Amatores.] See the Life of Alcibiades, c. 2. Apud Graecos, says Cic. de Rep. fragm. lib. iv., opprobrio fuit adolescentibus, si amatores non haberent. See Maximus Tyrius, Dissert, viii.----xi.; Potter's Antiq. of Greece, b. iv. c. 9.

6. † Nulla----vidua----quae non ad scenam eat mercede conducta.] This is not said with reference to that period in the history of Sparta when it adhered to the laws of Lycurgus, under which it was not allowed to witness either comedy or tragedy, as Plutarch in his Instituta Laconica shows, but to the time when the ancient discipline and austerity were trodden under foot, and the state sunk into luxury and effeminacy; a condition of things which took place under Leonidas and Agis, and chiefly, indeed, through the licentiousness of the women, if we may credit what Plutarch says in his life of Agis. From the earliest times, however, according to Aristotle, Polit. ii. 9, the Spartan women were inclined to live very intemperately and luxuriously, and Lycurgus endeavoured to subject them to laws, but was obliged to desist, through the opposition which they made. Hence Plato, also, de Legg. lib. ii., alludes to the a!nesij, laxity, of the Spartan women. ----Buchner. But with all such explanations the passage is still difficult and unsatisfactory. Why is a widow particularly specified? No passage in any ancient author has been found to support this observation of Nepos, if it be his. What Aristotle says in disparagement of the Lacedaemonian women is pretty well refuted, as Van Staveren observes, by Plutarch in his life of Lycurgus, c. 14. Besides, there were no female actors among the Greeks. For ad scenam Freinshemius (apud Boecler, ad h. l.) proposes to read ad coenam, which Gesner approves; Heusinger conjectures ad lenam. The conjecture of Withof, ad encaenia, compared with Hor. A. P. 232, Festis matrona moveri jussa diebus, might appear in some degree plausible, were not e0gkai/nia a word resting on scarcely any other authority than that of the Septuagint and ecclesiastical writers; for though it occurs in Quintilian, vii. 2, the passage is scarcely intelligible, and the reading has generally been thought unsound. Goerenz, ad Cic. de Fin. ii. 20, would read quae non ad coenam, eat mercede condictam, i.e. to a supper or banquet furnished by a general contribution of the guests. But none of these critics

cite any authority in support of their emendations. As to the last, it would be casting no dishonour upon a noble widow to say that she went to a coena condicta, for such coena might be among those of her own class. Nor is the applicability of mercede in such a phrase quite certain.

7. ‡ In scenam prodire et populo esse spectaculo, &c] Actors are here confounded with the rhapsodists, or reciters of poetry. Demosthenes, de Corona, upbraids Aeschines as being an actor.----Rinckii Prolegom. in Aem. Prob. p. xlii.

8. * This is not true of the Spartan women, for they, who boasted that they alone were the mothers of men, led a life of less restraint. Besides, by the laws of Lycurgus, the young women took part in the public exercises.----Rinck. Prolegom. ibid.

9. * Modestia.] "Good conduct," or "prudence," or "knowledge how to act," seems to be the true sense of the word. "Itaque, ut eandem [eu)taci/an] nos modestiam appellemus, sic definitur a Stoicis, ut modestia sit scientia earum rerum, quae agentur aut dicentur, suo loco collocandarum: ... scientia----opportunitatis idoneorum ad agendum temporum. Sed potest esse eadem prudentiae definitio."----Cic. de Off. i. 40.

10. † The Thracian Chersonese. But it is to be observed that the author, in this biography, confounds Miltiades, the son of Cimon, with Miltiades the elder, the son of Cypselus. It was the latter who settled the colony in the Thracian Chersonese, and left the sovereignty of it at his death to Stesagoras, the son of his half-brother Cimon, and brother to Miltiades the younger, who became governor of it on the death of Stesagoras, being sent out by Pisistratus for that purpose.

11. ‡ Ex his delecti Delphos deliberatum missi sunt, oui consulerent Apollinem, &c.] Either deliberatum, or qui consulerent Apollinem, might be emitted as superfluous. Bos retains both in his text, but suspects the latter.

12. * Cum delecta manu.] A body independent of those who were going to settle in the colony.

13. † Loca castellis idonea communiit.] A late editor absurdly takes castellis for a dative. Tacit. Ann. iii. 74: Castella et munitiones idoneis locis imponens.

14. * Dum ipse abesset.] He fixed, according to Herodotus, a term of sixty days for his absence, on the expiration of which the guardians of the bridge might depart.

15. † Principes.] The tyrants or sovereigns of the Greek cities, who held their power under the protection of Darius.

16. ‡ Se oppressa.] If he should be crushed, and the Persian empire consequently overthrown, they would be left without a protector.

17. * Civibus suis poenas daturos.] They would be called to account for having made themselves tyrants.

18. † The Ionians had rebelled against Persia, to which they had been subject, and, with some Athenians and Eretrians, had burned Sardis. This is alleged among the frivolous reasons for the Persian war. See Herod. v. 101-105; Perizon. ad Aelian. V. H. xii. 53; Fabric. ad Oros. ii. 8; and Plut. Vit. Aristid.---- Van Slaveren.

19. ‡ Omnes ejus gentis cives.] That is, all the people of Eretria in Euboea. They were carried to Susa, and treated kindly by Darius. See Herod. vi. 119.

20. § 9Hmerodro&moi, "day couriers," who could run a great distance in a day. Ingens die uno cursu emetientes spatium. Liv. xxxi. 24.

21. * The text is here in an unsatisfactory state, as all the critics remark, but I have given what is evidently the sense of the passage.

22. * Poiki/lh Stoa&, "the painted portico," as being adorned with pictures on subjects from Athenian history.

23. † Ad officium redire.] To submit again to the power of the Athenians.

24. ‡ Urbem.] The chief town of the island, bearing the same nama with it.

25. § See on Sall. Jug. c 37. The testudines were similar in construction and use to the vineae.

26. [Deterrerentur.] They feared the vengeance of the Persians if they submitted to Miltiades.

27. * Acharnanam civem.] This is the reading of most, if not all, of the MSS., and Bos retains it. "Aldus," says Bos, "was the first, I think, to change Acharnanam into Halicarnassiam, from having read in Plutarch that Neanthes said Halicarnassus in Caria was the birth-place of Themistocles's mother. For my part, I am unwilling to give up the old reading, especially as there is so much uncertainty on the point among writers." Some make Themistocles the son of a Thracian woman, and called her Abrotonus, some of a Carian, and called her Euterpe. See Plutarch. Themist. init. and Athenseus, xiii. 5. Acharnae was a borough of Attica. Plutarch, however, asserts that Themistocles was not of pure Attic blood on the mother's side. Nor is there any thing either in him or Athenaeus to support the reading Acharnanam.

28. * Bello Corcyraeo.] Rather Aeginetico, in the war with Aegina, as Lambinus and other commentators have observed; for that war happened about the time to which allusion is here made. See Herod. vii. 144, and Plutarch. Them. c. 4. But of a war with Corcyra neither Herodotus nor Thucydides makes any mention; a dispute between the Corcyreeans and Corinthians is noticed by Plutarch, Them. c. 24, which Themistocles, as arbiter, is said to have settled. The passage is therefore corrupt, perhaps from an error of Aemilius Probus, or perhaps Nepos himself made a mistake as to the name of the war.----Fischer.

29. † Largitione.] The money was divided, if we listen to Herodotus, vi. 46, 47; vii. 144, among the whole people, ten drachmae to every person of full-grown age.----Bos. But the division of it was the act of the people themselves, though it might be promoted by the influence of some of the leading men.

30. * Adeo angusto mari.] It was in the strait between the island of Salamis and the temple of Hercules, on the coast of Attica.----Bos.

31. † Interim.] The MSS. and editions are divided between interim and iterum. Bos prefers the former; Van Staveren the latter.

32. ‡ Pari modo.] Under the same circumstances as at Marathon a greater force being defeated by a smaller.

33. § Triplex Piraeei portus.] It is acutely shown by Bos that the Piraeeus was called triple from its containing three stations or basins, Cantharos, Aphrodision, and Zea.

34. * By public gods, deos publicos, are meant the deities worshipped throughout all the states of Greece, as Jupiter, Mercury, &c.; by national gods, patrios, such as were peculiar to Attica itself.

35. † Hospitium,] A mutual agreement to receive one another as guests. But according to Thucydides, i. 136, there was no such relation existing between them, for he speaks of Admetus as o!nta au)tw~| ou) fi/lon.

36. * Multo commodius.] This seems impossible. He might have better matter to produce, but surely not better language.

37. † Opsonium.] The word signifies all that was eaten with bread; all kinds of food besides bread.

38. ‡ Prope oppidum.] That is, near the city of Athens, where we learn from Pausanias that the tomb of Themistocles was to be seen in his time, in the reign of Marcus Antoninus.----Bos.

39. * Obtrectârunt inter se.] Diepoliteu&santo: they supported opposite parties in the state. So in the Life of Epaminondas, c. 5, it is said that he had Meneclides for an obtrectator. Such obtrectationes are called by Vell. Pat. ii. 43, civiles contentiones, and by Val. Max. iii. 8, acerrimi studii in administratione Reipublicae dissidia.----Gebhard. Plutarch says, that according to some there were dissensions between Aristides and Themistocles from their earliest years, so that in all their communications, whether on graver or lighter topics, the one always opposed the other.----Buchner.

40. † Abstinente.] That is, abstaining from the property of others; moderation; disinterestedness.

41. ‡ Priusquam poenâ liberaretur.] Before he was freed from the punishment (of exile).

42. * At the commencement of this chapter I have departed from Bos's text, and followed that of Freund and others, who make it begin with Quos quo facilius repellerent, &c.

43. * Plurima miscere.] To mingle, or throw into confusion, very many things.

44. † Book i. c. 128.

45. * Cum scytala.] The scytala was a staff, round which a slip of parchment being rolled obliquely, the orders of the Ephori were written on it longitudinally, so that, when unrolled, they could not be read until the parchment was again rolled round a staff of the same thickness, which the general had with him.

46. † More illorum.] That is, with extreme brevity.

47. * Regi.] Pausanias was not actually a king, but guardian to the young prince Pleistarchus, the son of Leonidas. Thucyd. i. 132.

48. † Argilius.] A native of Argilus, a town of Thrace on the Strymonic Gulf.

49. ‡ Amore venereo.] See the note on amatores in the preface.

50. § Vincula epistolae laxavit.] Letters were tied round with a string, which was sealed, probably, over the knot. The Argilian, according to Nepos, contrived to take off the string without breaking the seal, so that he might readily replace it.

51. * Quae Chalcioecos vocatur.] Whether the quae refers to aedem of Minervae, the critics are not agreed. Thucydides, i. 134, to_ i9ero_n th~j Xalkioi/kou, makes it apparent that it should be referred to Minerva. But Bos and Bremi concur in referring it to aedes.

52. * Neque legibus Atheniensibus emitti poterat.] Yet by Justin, ii. 15, Val. Maximus, v. 3 ext. 3, and v. 4 ext. 2, Seneca, Controvers. 24, and others, it has been said that Cimon's submission to go to prison was voluntary. Bos collects ample testimony to the contrary.

53. † See note on the preface.

54. * Hospitio.] See note on Themistocles, c. 8. Hospitium, might exist between two states, or between a state and a private individual, as well as between two individuals.

55. * Offensum fortuna.] That is, casu obvium, fortuito oblatum, "thrown in his way by chance," as Heusinger explains it in his note on the passage.----Fischer. This explanation is also approved by Boeclerus and Freinshemius. Lambinus erroneously interpreted it cui fortuna esset iniqua, and several others have trodden in his steps.

56. * Pervertere.] "Corrupt" is evidently the sense of pervertere in this passage, not "destroy," as some would make it. Lysander first endeavoured to corrupt the fidelity of the Thasians to the Athenians, and afterwards, when he found his endeavours unsuccessful, proceeded to use treachery and cruelty towards them.

57. * The account of Lysander's treachery to the Thasians is wanting in the manuscripts, but may be supplied from Polyaenus, i. 45. Those of the Thasians who had the greatest reason to fear Lysander, had fled to a temple of Hercules, which was held in the greatest veneration. At this temple Lysander called them all together to hear him address them, when he made them a speech full of the fairest promises of mercy and clemency. He said that he would think nothing of what was past; that no one had cause for fear or concealment; that they might all appear before him with full confidence in his good feelings towards them; and that he called Hercules, in whose temple they were, to witness that he spoke only what he meant. Having thus drawn them forth from their sanctuary, he, a few days after, when they were free from apprehension, fell upon them and put them to death. "He was guilty of a similar instance of perfidy at Miletus," says Bos, "as is also related by Polyaenus, and by Plutarch."

58. † Quàm verè de eo foret judicatum.] That is, how little he deserved acquittal.

59. * Librum graveni multis verbis.] "A heavy letter in many words."

60. * Dives; quum tempus posceret, &c.] This is Bos's reading. Many editions have Idem, quum tempus, &c.

61. † Non minus in vitâ quàm victu.] Bos and Boeder distinguish vita and victus in this manner; vita, they say, means a man's mode of living in public and among other men; victus his way of life at home, and diet at his own table. Cicero de Legg. iii. 14: Nobilium vita victuque mutato.

62. ‡ Privignus.] If we believe Diodorus Siculus, lib. xii, and Suidas, Alcibiades was the son of Pericles's sister. Hence Pericles is called his uncle by Val. Max, iii. 1, and Aul. Gell. xv. 17. Pericles appears, however, to have been the step-father of Alcibiades's wife, as Magius observes; for Alcibiades married Hipparete, the daughter of Hipponicus, whose wife Pericles afterwards espoused.----Bos.

63. * Omnes Hermae.] Mercury was reckoned the god of thieves, and therefore they used to erect his statues before their doors by way of prevention against the attempts of robbers and house-breakers.----Clarice.

64. † Itaque ille postea Mercurius Andocidis vocitatus est.] This is the reading of Bos and Van Staveren. Many other editions have, instead of these words, Andocidisque Hermes vocatus est.

65. ‡ Quod non ad privatam, sed ad publicam rem pertineret.] A manuscript of Boeder's has quae, but, as I suppose, from a fancy of the transcriber, who thought that the word must be a pronoun, referring to consensione, whereas it is a conjunction, showing the reason why "great dread was excited" by this occurrence "among the multitude," namely, because a union of many in the affair indicated a conspiracy, and must have respect to something of a public nature.----Bos.

66. § Mysteria.] The mysteries of Ceres; the Eleusinian mysteries.

67. * They thought that there was some conspiracy under the cloak of it.

68. † Consuetudinem.] Knowing the fickle character of the Athenians,

69. ‡ Crimine invidiae.] This is evidently the sense. Crimine invidiae for crimine invidioso.

70. § Licentia.] The license of the populace, which could scarcely be controlled.

71. * Ab hoc destitutus.] On the contrary, he was, according to Thucydides, viii. 49, 53, supported by Pisander.---- Bos.

72. * A considerable town of Aeolia. But it was at Notium, near Ephesus, not at Cyme, that the affair that caused the unpopularity of Alcibiades took place, through the folly of his lieutenant-general Antiochus, who, during his absence, brought on an engagement with Lysander, contrary to the express orders of Alcibiades.

73. † A city on the isthmus of the Thracian Chersonese. Most editions, previous to that of Bos, had Perinthus, from a conjecture of Longolius.

74. ‡ Primus Graeciae civitatis.] He was the first man of Greece that penetrated into that part of Thrace which was free, and where no colonies of Greeks had been established.----Fischer.

75. * Agere.] In its rhetorical sense, to state, plead, declare.

76. * Quem manu superari posse diffidebant.] "Whom they despaired would be able (i.e. whom they expected or thought would be unable) to be overcome by the hand."

77. † Emanus.] Bos would omit this word, as wanting authority.

78. * Matrem timidi flere non solere.] I have translated this according to the notion of Bremi, who says that timidus here means a cautious person, one who takes care of himself, and is on his guard against contingencies. Most translators have rendered it "the mother of a coward," &c., in which sense it would seem that the proverb was generally used.

79. † One of the minor harbours of Athens.

80. ‡ Quae ad victum pertinebant.] "Things which pertained to sustenance," i.e. provisions.

81. * Superioris more crudelitatis erant usi.] "Had used the manner of the former cruelty."

82. † Jugerum.] Though the juger or jugerum is generally rendered an acre, it in reality contained little more than half an acre. The juger was 240 feet long and 120 broad, containing therefore 28,800 square feet; the content of an English acre is 43,566 square feet.

83. ‡ Non propria esse consueverunt.] By propria, is meant "peculiarly one's own, and likely to continue so; appropriated to one's self." I have rendered it by "permanent;" most other translators have given something similar. Bos gives this remark about gifts to Nepos; other editors give it to Pittacus.

84. * Ex oppido.] The town was Aspendus, as appears from Xen. Hell. iv. 8, 30; Diod. Sic. xiv. 99.

85. * Apud quem ut multùm gratia valeret----effecit.] With whom he brought it to pass that he prevailed much by personal influence.

86. † What Nepos says here, as to the Lacedaemonians being persuaded by Tissaphernes to go to war with Persia, is scarcely reconcileable with fact, as Fischer observes, or with what is stated in the second chapter of the life of Agesilaus. Yet Schlegel and Wetzel, he adds, have made strong efforts to justify or excuse his statement. Thirlwall, however, seems to come nearer to the truth in his History of Greece, c. xxxv. The reader may also consult Smith's Biog. Dictionary, art. Tissaphernes.

87. ‡ Chiliarchum.] "Captain of a thousand." He is generally considered to have been chief of the life-guards, and to have been responsible, consequently, for the safety of the king's person.

88. * Sine hoc.] Some consider hoc masculine, referring to the chiliarchus.

89. * If this statement respecting Conon be true, his conduct in the matter is not to be reckoned among pia et probanda, "patriotic and deserving of praise." But it would appear from Diod. Sic. xiv. 85, and Xen. Hell. iv. 8, that the charge against him arose from envy on the part of Tithraustes and the other Persians.

90. † He was the father of Cleitarchus, who wrote a history of Alexander the Great's expedition. See Plin. H. N. x. 70. From what Pliny says of him, he seems to have been extremely credulous.

91. * Utrâque implicatus tyrannide Dionysiorum.] "Involved in," or "connected with, each tyranny of the Dionysii." For utroque Dionysio tyranno.

92. † Dionysius married two wives in the same day, Doris, a native of Locris, and Aristomache, the sister of Dion. But Dionysius the Younger was the son of Doris; so that, if Nepos is correct in saying that Sophrosyne was the daughter of Aristomache, he married his half-sister. See Plut. Vit. Dion. c. 3.

93. ‡ Dion, therefore, as Ernstius observes, married his own niece.

94. § Quae non minimum commendatur.] "Which is not in the lowest degree (i.e. which is in the highest degree) commended." Lambinus, from conjecture, read commendat, sc. hominem, which is more elegant (as Bos admits), and has been generally adopted by editors.

95. * Suorum causa.] For the sake of Aristomache and her children.

96. † Legationes.] Most editions have omnes after legationes. Bos and Van Staveren omit it.

97. ‡ Uni huic maxime indulgeret.] "He indulged him alone most "

98. § Ambitione.] Exquisito apparatu et ambitioso comitatu.----Gebhard. It was not, however, the elder, but the younger Dionysius, that received Plato with such ceremony. See Plato's Epist. 3 and 7; Plutarch, Vit. Dion., and Aelian, Var. Hist. iv. 18. Plato visited Sicily three times; the ostentatious reception occurred on the second occasion.

99. [Quippe quem venundari jussisset.] Bremi conjectures quippe qui eum, &c, which the sense indeed requires. Consult Plutarch, Vit. Dion., who, however, relates the matter a little differently. Lucian says that Plato was sent to a parasite, because he was ignorant of the parasite's art. See Diod. Sic. xv. 7; Diog. Laërt. iii. 18, 21.----Bos.

100. * That is, the portion of Italy, or Great Greece, which had been under the power of the elder Dionysius, part of which was still retained by his son.

101. † Lambinus first saw that we ought to read Dionysius, not Dion, Bos, Mosche, and most other editors, approve Lambinus's suggestion. Van Staveren omits the name altogether the sense being sufficiently clear without it.

102. * Ver. 204.

103. * Offensa in eum militum voluntate.] Yet Nepos says above, in this same chapter, that Dion "had gained the soldiery." Quum milites reconciliâsset, amitteret optimates.

104. * The ancients were accustomed, when they wished to devote themselves to prayer, or to do anything in private, to go up into the higher part of the house, or to keep a chamber in that part for that particular purpose. So Suetonius says of Augustus, c. 72, Si quando quid secreto aut sine interpellatione agere proposuisset, erat illi locus in edito sincularis. So Tacitus of Tiberius, Ann. vi. 21, Quoties super negotio Consultaret, edita domus parte utebatur.----Bos. He also refers to Judith, c. 8, and to Acts x. 9.

105. † Illi ipsi custodes.] The guards that had been stationed by Callicrates round Dion's house.

106. * Peltam pro parmâ fecit.] The pelta, was smaller than the parma, but both were smaller than the clypeus.----Bos.

107. * Apud Corinthum.] In the war generally called the Corinthian war, carried on by the Athenians, Thebans, and Argives, against the Lacedaemonians. See Diod. Sic. xiv. 86; Xen. Hell. iv. 4.

108. † From Xenophon, de Rep. Lacedaem., we learn that the mora consisted of 400 men; for it had four lochagi and eight pentecosteres.----Fischer. This seems to have been the regular and original number appointed by Lycurgus, but it varied afterwards according to times and circumstances. In the time of Xenophon (Hell. iv. 5) it appears to have consisted usually of

600. At other times it contained five, seven, or nine hundred. See Plutarch. Pelop. c. 17; Thucyd. v. 68, ibique Schol. Smith's Dict. of G. and R. Ant. art. Army, Greek.

109. † His name was Acoris; he had assisted Evagoras of Cyprus against Artaxerxes Mnemon. See Diod. Sic. xv. 29. He appears to have been the immediate predecessor of Nectanebis.

110. § Fabiani.] If the Roman soldiers were used to be called Fabians, which is an account given by none but our author, that I know of, it was occasioned by the gallantry of the Fabian family, that undertook to manage the war against the Vejentes by themselves, and were cut off, 300 of them in one battle.----Clarke. Others think that the name must have been derived from Fabius Cunctator. None of the better commentators say anything on the point.

111. * Nisi ejus adventus appropinquasset.] "Unless his approach, had been drawing near."

112. † The father of Philip, and grandfather of Alexander the Great. "This subject is more fully noticed by Aeschines de Fals. Leg. haud longe à principio."-----Bos. See Justin, vii. 4.

113. ‡ Bella Sociali.] A war in which Byzantium, Rhodes, Chios, and Cos leagued themselves against the Athenians, from their alliance with whom they had revolted. See Diod. Sic. xv. 78; xvi. 7, Ferizon. ad Aelian. Var. Hist. ii. 10. Comp. Life of Chabrias, c. 4.

114. * Phalanx is here used as a general term for a body of troops in close array.

115. † Artifices.] This word is here used in a very comprehensive sense, Including actors, musicians, and every other kind of public exhibitors.

116. ‡ Often written Nectanebis. "Diodorus Siculus has it either Nektenabw_j or Nektanebw&j."----Bos.

117. * A quitus magnas proedas Agesilaus rex eorum faciebat.] Attempts to interpret this passage have much exercised the ingenuity of the learned. Heusinger would have à quibus to signify "on whose side," or the same as pro quibus, but this Van Staveren justly rejects, and I, as well as he and Schmieder, doubt whether pro aliquo proedam facere can be regarded as good Latin. . . . For myself, I know not what to make of the passage, unless we receive the

cautious interpretation of Harles, Ithius, and Bremi, who understand proedam in a large or metaphorical sense for gain, presents, or a large sum of money, which Agesilaus either received from the Egyptians by agreement, or exacted from them, so that it might not improperly be regarded as proeda. Concerning the signification of this word, see Heyne ad Tibull. ii. 3, 38.----Fischer.

118. * See Life of Iphicrates, c. 3.

119. * Id----restituit.] Many editions, for id, have hanc, sc. pecuniam, but "id" says Bos, "for argentum or argentipondus, is perfectly correct."

120. † A prince of Thrace. Comp. Iphic. c. 3.

121. ‡ A strong city of the Propontis, on an island of the same name. It was besieged on this occasion, as Mitford supposes, by a force sent thither by Epaminondas, who was endeavouring to make Thebes a naval power to rival Athens.

122. § Satrap of Phrygia, who had revolted from Artaxerxes. "This war is mentioned by Demosthenes de Rhodior. Libertate."----Fischer.

123. [A city on the Hellespont, in the Thracian Chersonese, mentioned by Scylax, Stephanus de Urb., Strabo, and Pliny. The introduction of the name of this city into the text is due to Gebhard. Previously the common reading was Ericthonem, of which nobody knew what to make.

124. ¶ The Ionian Sea.

125. ** A pulvinus or pulvinar was a cushion, pillow, or bolster, and to support the arm or side of those who reclined on couches, like the bolsters on sofas in the present day. Pulvinar was afterwards used for the entire couch, on which the statues of the gods were placed on solemn occasions, as in the Roman lectisternia.

126. * That is, the cities on the Hellespont.

127. † *Cui oppositus Chares quum esset, non satis in eo praesidii putabatur.*] "To whom, when Chares had been opposed, there was not thought to be sufficient defence in him." Chares was a vain and ignorant braggart. See Diod. Sic. xvi. 86.

128. ‡ *In consilium.*] The words *quorum consilio uteretur*, which occur a little below, are not translated, as they appear, in the judgment of Bos and others, to be a mere interpolation.

129. § *Classem suppresserunt.*] Probably that they might not be driven on shore.

130. [It does not appear what place this was.

131. * *Jason tyrannus.*] He was tyrant of Pherae in Thessaly, and was, as it were, from his great power, king of the whole country. By calling him the "most powerful of all men," *omnium potentissimus*, Nepos seems to mean that he was more powerful than any single individual that had at that time to do with Greece.

132. † *De famâ.*] For his honour as a citizen. Conviction, on this occasion, would have subjected him, it appears, to loss of civil rights, or a)timi/a.

133. ‡ Unless we except Phocion, whose military character, however, was not very high.

134. * Pylaemenes was not killed by Patroclus, but by Menelaus; Hom. Il. v. 576.

135. † *Agresti duplici amiculo.*] Called *duplex* because it was thick and stout, woven of thread of a double thickness; or because it was made of cloth doubled. The Greeks called it xlai–na diplh~.----Fischer. A modern annotator thinks that *duplica* refers to the "folding" of the cloak as it was worn, not to the "texture!"

136. * *Qui tantum quod ad hostes pervenerat..*] This reading is an emendation of Lambinus, and it is extremely doubtful whether it ought to have been so favourably regarded by Van Steveren and Bos, who have admitted it into their texts. Some of the manuscripts have *qui dum ad hostes pervenerat*. Heusinger thinks we might read *tantum qui dum*, or *qui tantum*

dum, tantum dum, being a form of expression similar to vixdum, nondum. The Ed. Ultraject. has qui tantum non ad, &c. Most of the older common editions have qui nondum ad, &c.

137. * Cilciae vortae.] A pass so called.

138. † A body of soldiery among the Persians, mentioned by Strabo, Plutarch, Arrian, Pausanias, and others. Hesychras thinks that they had their name from some place or tribe.

139. ‡ Captianorum. A people unknown to geographers. Schottus suggested that we should read, with a slight alteration, Caspianorum, people from the borders of the Caspian sea.---- Bos. Bos, on the whole, approves this suggestion.

140. * Quibus fretus.] I have given the quibus that sense which it evidently requires.

141. † Peace and friendship with himself, preparatory to his being received into favour by the kiag. This is Nipperdey's explanation. Other editors have merely complained of the apparent tautology in

142. * A rege missam.] These words are wanting in some editions. The king presented his right hand to some person, in order that that person might present his own to Mithridates in the king's name.

143. *. In vitiis poni.] "Is accounted among disparagements, disgraces, or vices."

144. † A plurimis omnium anteponuntur virtutibus.] "Are by many preferred to the best qualities of all." Many would rather hear of the actions than of the virtues of eminent men.

145. ‡ Damon was an Athenian, mentioned by Plutarch de Musicâ, Plato, de Rep., lib. iv., and Athenaeus, xiv. 11. Lamprus is also noticed by Plutarch in the same treatise, by Plato in his Menexenus, and by Athenœus, i. 16, ii. 2. Damon is said to have taught Pericles, and Lamprus Sophocles.

146. § Tibiis.] See the note on this word in the preface.

147. [See Cic. de Orat. III. 34; Off. i 4; Diod. Sic. lib. vi. in Exc. Peiresc. p. 247; Pausanias, ix. 13; Aelian, V. H. iii. 17; Porphyr. Vit. Pythag. extr.; Jamblich. Vit. Pythag. c. 35. ... A letter of his to a certain Hipparchus is among the Epistles of the Greeks published by Aldus, and also among the fragments of the Pythagoreans added by Casaubon to Diogenes Laertius.---- Bos.

148. * Tristem et severum senem in familiaritate antepossuerit.] "He preferred a grave and austere old man in familiarity," i. e. as an associate.

149. † Levia et potius contemnenda.] The study of philosophy, at least in the time of Nepos, was not numbered by the Romans among despicable pursuits.

150. ‡ Ad eum finem quoad, &c.] Ad eum finem, as Bos observes, is the same as usque eo.

151. * Multis millibus versuum.] "In many thousands of verses." Versus was used by the Roman as well for a line in prose as for a line in poetry.

152. † Indidem Thebis.] That is, "from the same place, Thebes."

153. ‡ Castris est vobis utendum, non palaestra.] That is, you must give your serious attention to the one more than to the other. You may in the palaestra inure yourselves to exercise; but you must remember that your thoughts are to be directed beyond the palaestra to the camp.

154. * Hic.] Some read huic, "to him."

155. † The argument of Epaminondas, in these observations, is this, referring properly only to Orestes and Oedipus: that they were born, it must be granted, the one at Argos, and the other at Thebes, but that, as they were born innocent, neither of those cities can be blamed merely for having been their birth-place; after they were polluted with crimes, however, and were in consequence expelled from their native cities, they were received by the Athenians, who, by sheltering them, might be considered to have become partakers in their guilt.

156. ‡ Legati ante pugnam Leuctricam.] These words are rejected by Longolius, Magius, Lambinus, and Schottus, as a gloss that has intruded itself from the margin into the text. But as they are found in the best copies, Bos, who cannot but suspect them, is content with including them in brackets.

157. * This was the army that was sent into Thessaly to rescue Pelopidas from Alexander of Pherae. See Diod. Sic. xv. 71, 72.

158. † He had been accused of treachery, and the people in consequence had taken from him his Boiwtarxi/a, and reduced him to a private station. Diod. Sic. ibid.

159. ‡ Saepius.] Nepos mentions, however, only two occasions; and no more are discoverable from other authors.

160. * Collegae ejus.] His colleagues and himself.

161. † In periculo suo.] The word periculum, in this passage, greatly perplexed the old commentators; no one could find any satisfactory sense for it; and various conjectures were offered as to a substitute for it. At last Gebhard suggested that the passage might be interpreted "Epaminondam petiisse, ut in actis illis, in quibus suum periculum ad memoriam notetur, talia inscriberent," so that periculum, in his opinion, would be the same as "adnotatio sive commemoratio periculi illius in tabulis publicis," the record of his periculum in the public registers. Schoppius, Verisim. iv. 18, went farther, and said that periculum signified "libellum sive annalem publicum." This interpretation was adopted by Bos and Fischer, and subsequently by Bremi and others, and is approved by Gesner in his Thesaurus sub voce. Tzschucke interprets it elogium damnationis, or scripta judicii sententia.

162. ‡ Messene constituta.] He settled or built (e!ktise) Messene, and brought many colonists to it, says Diod. Sic. xv. 66. See Pausan. ix. 14, atque alibi.

163. * Quod liberos non relinqueret.] These words, in most editions, are placed lower down, after consulere diceret, where Lambinus was the first to put them. Bos suspects that they may be altogether spurious.

164. * Apud Cadmaeam.] The citadel of Thebes, said to have been founded by Cadmus.

165. † Aliena paruisse imperio.] By these words it is not signified that Thebes was actually subject to any other power, but that it always held a secondary place.

166. ‡ Phoebidas was sent to assist Amyntas, king of Macedonia, who was going to besiege Olynthus with the aid of his allies the Lacedaemonians, because its inhabitants had refused to make satisfaction to him. See Diod. Sic. xv. 19.----Fischer.

167. § Per Thebas.] This is evidently the sense.

168. * See Epaminondas, c. 10.

169. † Ut quemque ex proximo locum fors obtulisset, eo patriam recuperare niterentur.] "Opportunity" seems to be the sense of locus in this passage, as in Hamilc. c. 1, locus nocendi. Quemque is for quemcumquei as Van Staveren remarks.

170. * Tempus et dies.] Charon had not only settled the day, but the time of the day.----Bos.

171. † Sejunctum ab re positâ.] By res, "the subject," we must understand the life of Pelopidas. Yet no apology was necessary for introducing the remark, as it is extremely applicable to the enterprise which Nepos is relating.

172. ‡ Hierophante.] A hierophantes was one who understood and could interpret religious mysteries. Archias was high-priest of the Eleusinian rites of Ceres.

173. * See Epaminondas, c. 8.

174. * In comitio.] A Latin word used by the author for the Greek, which would be e0forei=n, the court of the Ephori.

175. † Quod iter Xerxes anno vertente confecerat.] Anno vertente, sc. se, "a year turning itself or revolving," i.e. in the course of a year, in a full year. In the Life of Themistocles, however, c. 5, Xerxes is said to have made the journey in six months.

176. * Supplicibus eorum.] Whether eorum refers to barbaros, which is nearer to it, or to deorum, which is farther from it, has been a question among the commentators. Bos refers it to deorum, and I think him right. A recent editor imagines that it is to be referred to simulacra arasque. Magius would read deorum instead of eorum, and his suggestion is approved by Bremi and Buchung.

177. † This appears to be an error; for Xenophon, Ages. 7, 5, and Plutarch, Vit. Ages, speak of Agesilaus as having heard about the battle; and it is therefore to be concluded, as Magius and Lambinus observe, that he was not present in it, but that it took place while he was on his march homeward.

178. ‡ Ab insolentia gloriae.] "From the presumptuousness of boasting."

179. * Quo ne proficisceretur----exire noluit.] The conclusion of the sentence does not suit the commencement of it. It is a decided anacoluthon, as Harles, Bremi, and Bardilis observe.

180. † Nisi ille fuisset, Spartam futuram non fuisse.] "Unless he had been, Sparta would not have been."

181. ‡ Aucto numero eorum qui expertes erant consilii.] Bos suggests this explanation of the passage: that only a part of those who occupied the height intended to go over to the enemy, and designed, by force or persuasion, to bring over the others qui expertes erant consilii; but were deterred from doing so when the number of the true men was strengthened by the followers of Agesilaus. Bos, however, suggests at the same time, that we might read aucti numero eorum, which Bremi is inclined to adopt.

182. * Among whom were Tachos of Egypt, and Mausolus, king of Caria, from both of whom he received large presents; as he did also, probably, from Cotys and Autophradates. See Xen. Ages. 2, 26, 27.

183. † Huc.] That is, on the straw.

184. * Nectanabis II., nephew of Tachos, whom he dethroned with the aid of Agesilaus.

185. † Portum qui Menelai vocatur.] On the coast of Marmorica.

186. ‡ Cyrenae, -arum, or Cyrene, -es, but the latter is the far more common form.

187. * Cardianus.] Cardia was a town in the Thracian Chersonese, on the gulf of Mêlas.

188. † Multo honorificentius.] Because freedmen and slaves, for the most part, purchased the office of scribe or secretary among the Romans with money, as is observed by Casaubon in Capitolin. Vit. Macrini, c. 7, and by Lipsius, Elect. i. 32.----Loccenius. At Athens, however, Samuel Petit, Comm. in Leges Atticas, 1. iii. tit. 2, shows that the office of scribe was as little honourable as it was at Rome.-----Bos. Such was doubtless the case throughout Greece a few of the more eminent secretaries might be held in esteem and respect, but the majority would be of just the same standing as at Rome.

189. * 9Etairikh_ i3ppoj, about a thousand or twelve hundred of the flower of the Macedonian cavalry. The name is from e3tairoj, a friend or companion, either because they were united with one another as friends, or because they were associates or companions of the king.

190. † Tradita esset tuenda eidem-- Perdiccae.] "Was committed, to be taken care of, to the same Perdiccas."

191. ‡ In suam tutelam pervertissent.] Should come "to their own guardianship," should be out of their minority, and no longer under the guardianship of others.

192. § Industriam.

193. * A distinguished officer in the army of Alexander, after whose death he had the government of Phrygia on the Hellespont.

194. † Ad internecionem.] Properly, "to the utter destruction" of one of the two contending parties.

195. ‡ Antipater, Craterus, and their supporters.

196. * A Seleuco et Antigono.] For Antigono it is now generally supposed that we should read Antigene, Antigenes being mentioned by Diod. Sic. xviii. 59, as one of the leaders of the Argyraspides; another being Teutamus. Antigenes was the first to attack Perdiccas, as Van Staveren observes, referring to Arrian apud Photium, p. 224. The same critic suggests that we might even, with some probability alter Seleuco into Teutamo, but does not wish to press this conjecture

197. † Plaga.] Meaning the death of Perdiccas.

198. * Callidum fuit ejus inventum, quemadmodum, &c.] "It was an ingenious contrivance of his, how the animal might be warmed," &c.

199. † Caput.] Not only the head, however, but all the fore-part of the body must have been tied up, the strap being passed round the body behind the fore-legs.

200. * In principiis.] See note on Florus, iii. 10, Bonn's Cl. Library. Eumenes, to give effect to this device, pretended, as Polyaenus tells us, to have received directions from the spirit of Alexander, which had appeared to him in a dream. It is strange that the Macedonian officers should have allowed themselves to be so deluded.

201. * De rebus summis.] "Of their chief concerns."

202. † Non minus totidem dierum spatio.] "Not less than the space of just as many days."

203. * Fructum oculis capere.] "To gain gratification for their eyes."

204. † Ut deuteretur.] The word deutor is not found elsewhere. It seems not to be the same with abutor, as some suppose, but to have much the same sense as the simple verb. But most editions have se uteretur, an alteration of Lambinus.

205. * This is so little of a reason for Eumenes' success against his opponents in the field, that Buchner, Bos, and others, suppose that some words have been lost out of the text.

206. * The sentence begins with Sic Eumenes, and ends with talem habuit exitum vitae, a fault similar to that which has been noticed in Ages. c. 6.

207. † Memoria est nulla.] That is, no one thinks of praising his military exploits equally with his moral virtues.

208. * Quum adversus Charetem eum subornaret.] I have given to subornaret the sense to which Bos thinks it entitled. To what part of Phocion's life this passage relates is uncertain. Bos refers to Plutarch, Phocion, c. 14, where it is stated that Phocion was sent to Byzantium with a force to accomplish what Chares had failed in doing. But no mention is made there of any support given to Phocion by Demosthenes.

209. * Capitis damnatos.] That is, made atimous, or infamous, deprived of civil rights, and condemned, perhaps, in addition, to exile or death.

210. † Philip Aridaeus, the half brother and nominal successor of Alexander the Great.

211. ‡ An Athenian demagogue, who was put to death by the people of Athens soon after the death of Phocion.

212. * Undecim viris.] Eleven petty officers, whose duty was to see the sentences of the law put in execution.

213. † Namque huic uni contigit, quod nescio an nulli.] I have endeavoured to give a satisfactory turn in the English to that which is not very satisfactory in the Latin. "For (that) happened to (him) alone, (of) which I know not whether (it happened) to any one (else)." If it

happened to him alone, it of course happened to no one else. Some editors read ulli: but nulli appears to be the right reading, nescio an being taken in the sense of "perhaps."

214. * A barbaris.] The Carthaginians, when they were at war with the elder Dionysius.

215. † Soror ex iisdem parentibus nata.] She was whole sister to him and Timophanes.

216. * Fana deserta.] Bos retains deserta, in his text, but shows an inclination, in his note, to adopt the emendation of Lambinus, deleta; déserta, however, which is found, I believe, in all the manuscripts, is susceptible of a very good interpretation; for temples that were deserted or neglected might have fallen into decay, and require to be repaired or rebuilt.

217. * In theatrum.] Public assemblies were often held in theatres.

218. † Sacellum Au)tomati/aj.] A word compounded of au)toj, self, and ma&w, to desire or will, and applied to Fortune as acting from her own will or impulse.

219. * Se voti esse damnatum.] The meaning is, that he was now obliged to the fulfilment of that which he had vowed when he prayed for such a degree of freedom.

220. † Timoleonteum.] Sc. Gymnasium.

221. ‡ Graecae gentis.] All the preceding biographies are those of Greeks, except that of Datames.

222. § Separatem sunt relatae.] In another book written by Nepos, which contained the lives of kings, as Lambinus thinks; and Vossius de Hist. Lat. i. 14, is of the same opinion. I rather imagine that the writings of other authors, who have spoken of the acts of kings, are intended; for if Nepos had meant a composition of his own, he would have said à me sunt relatae, as in the Life of Cato, c. 3, he says in eo libra quem separatim de eo fecimus.----Bos.

223. * Macrochir, Longimanus, or "long-handed." Mnemon, mnh&mwn, signifying one that has a good memory.

224. † There was no remarkable proof of his justice given on this occasion. His mother Parysatis poisoned his wife Statira; but he spared Parysatis, and put to death Gingis, who had merely been her tool. See Plutarch, Life of Artaxerxes, c. 19.

225. ‡ Morbo naturae debitum reddiderunt.] "Paid (their) debt to nature by disease."

226. * Nunquam hosti cessit.] Not exactly true; but he doubtless resisted the enemy vigorously.

227. † Erycem.] Not the mountain, as Bos observes, but the town situated between the top and the foot of the mountain, of both of which the Romans had possession. See Polyb. i. 53; ii. 7, Diod. Sic. xxiv. 2; Cluverius, Sicil. Antiq. ii. 1.

228. ‡ Three islands on the western coast of Sicily. This battle brought the first Punic war to an end.

229. * Son of Demetrius, and last king but one of Macedonia. See Justin, xxviii. 4; xxix. 1-4; xxx. 3; xxxii. 2.

230. † A Rubro Mari.] It is the Mare Erythraeum that is meant, lying between Arabia and India.

231. * Saltum Pyrenaeum.] The forest, i. e. the woody chain or range of the Pyrenees.

232. † Clastidio.] Clastidio, thus given by Bos, without a preposition or any word to govern it, cannot be right. It seems necessary either to read Clastidii, or, with Lambinus, de Clastidio. I have adopted the latter, as the termination in o is found in all the manuscripts. But no account of a battle between Hannibal and Scipio at Clastidium (a town of Gallia Cispadana, at no great distance from the Po), is found in any other author. Ithe has therefore ventured, somewhat boldly, to eject Clastidio from his text altogether.

233. * Quo repentino objectu viso.] "Which sudden appearance being seen" by the Romans.

234. * Absens----sustulit.] The battle being fought by one of Hannibal's generals in his absence.

235. † Circiter millia passuum trecenta.] One hundred and fifty miles is supposed to be nearer the truth.

236. * A town on the Liris, in the Volscian territory.

237. † Praetor.] This office seems, from what follows, to have been in a great degree financial; but judicial duties were probably combined in it.

238. ‡ Rex.] The two annual magistrates at Carthage were called suffetes in the Punic tongue; the Greeks and Romans called them kings.

239. * Antiochus here suffered a defeat from the Romans.

240. † In Pamphylio mari.] The sea on the coast of Pamphylia in Asia Minor.

241. ‡ Antiocho fugato.] Viz., in the battle near Magnesia, at the bottom of Mount Sipylus in Lydia.

242. § Principibus praesentibus.] Many of the old editions have Gortyniis praesentibus, a manifest error, as Bos observes. Principibus occurs in three manuscripts.

243. * Illud recusavit, ne id a se fieri postularent.] "He refused this, (requesting) that they would not require that to be done by him."

244. * Cato the censor, the great grandfather of the Cato that killed himself at Utica.

245. † Situate about ten miles south-east of Rome, not far from the modern Frascati.

246. † Aedilis plebis.] There were two sorts of aediles, plebeian and curule.

247. * Privatus in urbe mansit.] That is, he did not take any other foreign province. Plutarch, however, in his life of Cato, says that Scipio was appointed to succeed Cato in Spain, but that, being unable to procure from the senate a vote of censure on Cato's administration, he passed his term of office in inactivity.

248. † Edictum.] The code of regulations which a magistrate published on entering upon his office, adopting what he chose from the edicts of his predecessors, and adding what he thought proper of his own. See Adam's Rom. Ant. p. 111, 8vo. ed.

249. ‡ Circiter annos octoginta.] This passage is in some way faulty. Bos thinks that the number is corrupt, or that the three words have been intruded from the margin into the text. Pighius would read Vixit circiter annos octoginta, et, &c.

250. § A multis tentatus.] Plutarch, in his life of Cato, c. 15, says that Cato was attacked or accused about fifty times in the sourse of his political life.----Bos.

251. * Ab origine ultima stirpis Romanae.] "From the most remote origin of the Roman race." His family was so old that it reached back to the earliest age of Rome.

252. * Versuram facere.] Versura, according to Festus süb voce, properly signifies borrowing from one to pay another. Our language has no word corresponding to it.

253. † Septem modii.] This is the reading of the old editions, and of the manuscripts of Manutius, Gifanius, Schottus, Leid, and Medic. 2. But since it appears from Cicero in Verr. iii. 45, 46, 49, as well as from Ausonius, Suidas, and other ancient writers, that the medimnus contained six modii, Manutius, Faernus, and Ursinus, following Georg. Agricola de Mens. et Pond. Gr. et Rom. lib. ii., substituted sex for septem in this passage, and Lambinus, with all the subsequent editors of Nepos, adopted it. There seem, however, to have been variations in

the content of the medimni and modii. According to the old author on measures, published by Rigaltius among the Auctores Finium Regundorum, p. 335, five modii made a medimnus; and Isidore, Orig. xvi. 25, makes the same statement . . . . . Phavorinus, again, says that the medimnus was mo&dioi e(pta.----Bos. On the whole, therefore, Bos prefers that septem should stand. The modius was 1 gal. 7.8576 pints English.

254. * Phidiae.] Some editions have Piliae. "This was some Phidias, who, though unmentioned by any other writer, was known to Nepos through Atticus with whom he was intimate." See c. 13.---- Van Staveren.

255. * About £1600 of our money.

256. † About £80,729 3s. 4d.

257. * Optimarum partium.] Ursinus and Schottus conjecture optimatum partium.---- Heusinger thinks optimarum right.

258. † Ad hastam publicam nunquam, accessit.] That is, to a sale of the property confiscated in the proscriptions. A hasta, or spear, set up, was the signal of an auction; a custom derived from the sale of spoils taken in war.

259. † Nullius rei neque praes, neque manceps factus est.] The farmers, mancipes, of the revenues were chiefly equités, but Atticus, though of that order, neither became a farmer himself, nor a surety, praes, for any farmer.

260. § Neque suo nomine neque subscribens.] He neither brought accusations against people himself, nor supported the accusations of others by setting his hand to them. This is said with reference to the time of the proscriptions.

261. [That he declined offices generally is stated above in this chapter; there is no particular mention that he declined the praetorship.

262. * Ejus observantia.] Observantia, as Bos and Fischer observe, is evidently to be understood actively.

263. † Secutum est illud, occiso Caesare, &c.] The commencement of this chapter is extremely bald. Whether tempus, which Bos understands with illud, has dropped out of the text, or whether the author purposely omitted it, must remain doubtful. Perhaps more words than one are lost.

264. ‡ Penes Brutos.] Some editions have Brutum. I prefer the plural, says Bos, Marcus and Decimus being meant.

265. * Dicis----causa.] Bos's text, and many others, with all the manuscripts, have necis causa. Dicis causa is a conjecture of Cujacius. Necis is defended by Savaro, who says that the provinces were given to Brutus and Cassius for killing Caesar. Gebhard supports Savaro, referring to Vell. Pat. ii. 62: Bruto Cassioque provinciae, quas jam ipsi sine ullo senatus consulto occupaverant, decretae. Bos, too, quotes from. Appian, 9H boulh_ ge/ra toi=j a)nelon~sin w(j turannokto&noij e0yhfi/zeto. But, as Ernstius observes, the provinces could not have been given to Brutus and Cassius particularly for killing Caesar, for they were not the only ones concerned in his death; and he therefore prefers dicis causa, supposing that the provinces were given to them merely to afford them an honourable pretext for leaving the city to avoid the fury of the lower orders. Heusinger not unhappily conjectures necessitatis causa.

266. † £807 5s. 10d.

267. ‡ £2421 17s. 6d.

268. § A war that arose between Mark Antony and Octavius (see Florus, iv. 4), through a dispute about the will of Caesar, in which Octavius had been set before Antony, who, in displeasure, had recourse to arms, and besieged Decimus Brutus, who took the side of Octavius, in Mutina, now Modena.----Fischer.

269. [Divinatio.] We should rather read divinitas, as Buchner first observed. Divinatio occurs below, c. 16, but in its proper sense.

270. * Commendationem.] Manuscripts and editions are divided between this word and commoditatem.

271. † Stiterit vadimonium.] Promittere vadimonium is to give bail for one's appearance in court on a certain day; sistere or obire vadimonium is to appear according to the obligation entered into when the bail was given.

272. ‡ Versuram facere.] See note on c. 2.

273. § Ille autem sui judicii----intuebatur, &c.] The words sui judicii must be taken as a genitive of the quality, Ille autem, cum vir esset sui judicii, &c. But they are, as they stand, by no means satisfactory: something seems to be wanting in the text. Schottus, however, thinks them an intruded gloss.

274. * Imperatorum.] The triumvirs, Caesar, Antony, and Lepidus. At their approach he retired from the forum, i.e., from all public business.

275. * Where Atticus had estates. See c. 14.

276. † Neque tamen priùs ille fortunam, quàm se ipse, finxit.] A very inapplicable observation. Nepos first says that a man's manners fashion his fortune, and then speaks of Atticus forming himself and his fortune. The word tamen would intimate some opposition; but there is none. Atticus, having formed his manners, might leave his manners to form his fortune.

277. * Nisi in deprecandis amicorum aut periculis aut incommodis.] "Unless in deprecating either the dangers or troubles of his friends."

278. † Domum Tamphilanam.] To what Tamphilus the house had belonged is not known. There were two consuls with that surname, A.U.C. 570, 571.

279. * Plus salis.] The word salis does not admit of a very satisfactory explanation in this passage. Most interpreters, says Boecler, take it for gratia, venustas, ars, elegantia.

280. † Pedissequus.] The word signifies any slave or servant who follows or attends on his master; a footman, lacquey, or page. Many of the better sort of slaves, among the Romans, were so well educated that, while they still continued pedissequi, they were able to act as anagnostae or librarii, readers or transcribers.

281. † Artifices caeteri.] Workmen of all kinds.

282. § Terna millia ceris.] Such is the reading of all the manuscripts and editions, but no commentator has thought it a sufficient sum. It amounts only to £24 4s. 4 1/2d. Hotomannus, Tract. de Re Nummaria, p. 87, would read tricena, thirty, but even £240 a month would be a very small expenditure for a man of such income as Atticus. Conjecture, however, in such a case, is useless.

283. * Allud acroama] Acroama, as Fischer observes, generally signified among the Latins, not a thing, but a person; and it may be so interpreted in this passage.

284. † In sestertio vicies.] £16,145 16s. 8d.

285. ‡ In sestertio centies.] £80,729 3s. 4d

286. § Religiose promittebat.] He made no promise lightly, but as if he were religiously determined to fulfil it.

287. * Omnia negotia.] This must be taken with much limitation; he might do all the business with which they troubled him.

288. † Nunquam cum matre in gratiam rediisse.] Never having had any disagreement with her.

289. * Ornavit.] Bos, Vossius, and others, prefer ordinavit. But Hensinger thinks ornavit may very well be taken in the sense in which I have rendered it.

290. * Conciliare fortunam.] "Procure him his fortune," make his fortune. As the mores are, so the fortune will be.

291. † Dignitate pari.] It is evidently dignity of birth that is intended.

292. * In unum intestinum.] Barthius wished to alter it to imum intestinum, because, I suppose, he knew that there was the seat of the disease. . . . But there is no need of change; unum is the same as solum.----Bos.

293. * Temporibus superesse.] The commentators are not agreed about the exact sense of these words. I follow Heusinger, who understands them in the sense of "getting over, and surviving, the troubles and danger of the present time."

294. † A.U.C. 720; B.C. 34.

295. ‡ Comitantibus omnibus bonis.] This omnibus, like the omnia in c. 15, must be understood in a limited sense.

296. The following text, and the notes to it, are not found in the Bohn text, and have been added to the public domain online edition. I have located the Latin text in the Loeb edition, and made a public domain translation from them. Robert Stonehouse in humanities.classics kindly made a translation of fragment V, which I have also consulted.

297. This comes from the Codex Gif., according to Savaro and Patavius.

298. On the first page of the Codex Guelferbytanus Gudianus 2788, saec. xiii, of Cicero's Philippics. Apparently formed part of the preface of the book De Historicis Latinis.

299. I.e., history.

300. From Lactantius, Inst. Div. iii.15.10. The dots indicate a lacuna in the Latin. Other brief quotations from Nepos may be found, I gather, in Suetonius and Aulus Gellius.

Made in the USA
Coppell, TX
07 February 2021